Bwls

Making the Most of Your Game

Patrick Hulbert

ROBERT HALE • LONDON

© Patrick Hulbert 2014
First published in Great Britain 2014

ISBN 978-0-7198-1297-2

Robert Hale Limited
Clerkenwell House
Clerkenwell Green
London EC1R 0HT

www.halebooks.com

A catalogue record for this book is available from the British Library

2 4 6 8 10 9 7 5 3 1

Typeset by Eurodesign
Printed in China

To Dad

Contents

Acknowledgements

First and foremost, I would like to thank Robert Hale publishers and Alexander Stilwell in particular for commissioning this book. The sport of bowls will hopefully benefit from the publication of this work.

I would like to thank Mum, who with Dad, got me into the game of bowls, and I would like to thank posthumously John Kilyon – a great Leicestershire stalwart and England international whom I looked up to immensely as a young, aspiring player. It was because of John that I learnt temperament is key.

Thanks also to my brothers Matthew and Tim, who played with me for years and showed me how to behave on the rink (and occasionally how not to).

Thanks are also due to those who assisted in the production of this book.

The bowlers Rex Hazeldine, Tony Allcock MBE, David Bryant CBE, Willie Wood MBE, Andy Thomson MBE, Steve Glasson OAM, John Rednall, Natalie Melmore, John McGuinness and David Rhys Jones, who kindly contributed in the writing of this book, all love the sport and are great ambassadors for our game; their input to this book is greatly appreciated.

The input of Professor Ian Maynard of Sheffield Hallam University, an expert in the field of sport psychology, has been integral to the message of the book. Thinking outside the box and using advice from professionals away from the sport of bowls gives us all a chance to improve our grasp of how to push on and progress within the sport by taking fundamental psychological practices and implementing them in our game.

I would like to thank Key Publishing Limited, the owners of *Bowls International* magazine, and in particular consultant editor Paul Hamblin, for allowing me to write the book in the first place and to use input from a few of the contributors of *Bowls International* magazine and some images from our library.

A particular thanks goes once more to Willie Wood and Andy Thomson for allowing me to photograph them, and to Potters Resort, where many of the pictures were taken. Many thanks also go to former England junior international James Alcock for pictorial help in the physical section of the book at Charnwood Indoor Bowls Club.

Finally, I would like to thank the readers of this book. I hope it helps you improve your game, and I really do think that it will.

Introduction

I am not the greatest bowler in the world. I never have been and I can probably guarantee that I never will be. I am not a qualified coach either – if you want a bowls book written solely by someone who is a 'coach' or has won 250 world titles then this book is not for you. Put it back on the shelf. However, if you want a comprehensive yet concise, practical and engaging piece of work that will aid you to become a better bowler and teach you key skills to help you be a good team member, then keep reading.

Well, what am I then? I feel I have many traits that have enabled me to play at the highest level at county standard and represent the England under-25 side as one of the longest-ever serving players in the country's history – patience, hard work, determination, coolness under pressure and, most importantly, a good team ethic have allowed me to play in some of the most exciting and high-quality matches one could wish to play in, and with and against some of the best players.

I do not profess to possess all the answers to make you the superstar bowler of the world. If I had all the answers then I would be a regular senior international with a 'perfect' delivery. For this reason, I will also be getting help in this book from some of the greatest stars of the game. You *will* get input from players with a vast array of world titles after all. Their invaluable contribution, accompanied by my knowledge of the sport, has ensured that this book is the most rounded and comprehensive (yet concise) bowls book available on the market.

With help from Tony Allcock MBE, an eighteen times World Champion, Willie Wood MBE, the 'Peter Pan' of bowls with a whole host of World and Commonwealth medals, three times world indoor singles champion Andy Thomson MBE, Bowls Australia Head Coach Steve Glasson OAM, Commonwealth Games singles champion Natalie Melmore and, arguably the greatest bowler who ever lived, David Bryant CBE – just some of the star names contributing to this book – this is your 'one-stop-all' book on bowls and some-thing that has never been attempted before on this scale. Google each of the contributors to this book and see just what they have achieved in the sport and in their professional careers – it is truly incredible!

I am going to focus on five major areas and approaches to ensure you can improve on every aspect of your game. Thus, the main areas I will scrutinize will be the technical, psychological, tactical, teamwork, and physical aspects in the sport of bowls, and I will be rounding off with a conclusion, looking at how to blend all of these elements to make the 'perfect bowler' – so it comes as no surprise that the model for this 'perfect bowler' comes in the shape of David Bryant CBE.

I am probably ten years ahead of the game with regard to my focus on the physical side of the sport of bowls. I may even be twenty years ahead. I may have missed the point completely – but I very much doubt it and I hope that elements in this book will pioneer a different approach towards physical aspects that will aid you in the sport of bowls.

Furthermore, psychology is seen nowadays as an essential aspect in any sport. Football teams, for example, all have their own sports psychologists and more emphasis is being put on this. However, psychological 'analysis' in the sport of bowls usually tends to be about a blinkered notion of a player either having 'bottle', or not having the nerve necessary when under pressure. This book will aid you to prepare for matches appropriately and give sugges-tions to assist you to go into a match with a positive frame of mind. This second section will also delve into the finer details of how to play in a partic-ular position and the mindset needed for that task.

With regard to the psychological aspects of bowls, in addition to asking top players for their input, I have also included some invaluable content from Professor Ian Maynard of Sheffield Hallam University, a sports psychology expert.

For the physical section, I have relied heavily on Rex Hazeldine, a lecturer at Loughborough University and currently the Bowls England sports scientist. Rex is in the Sports Coach UK Hall of Fame for his work in numerous sports and is a fully qualified coach in the sport of bowls. His knowledge about phys-ical exercises to improve performance and reduce the risk of injury in bowls is something innovative and fresh-thinking in what can sometimes be consid-ered a conservative and narrow-minded sport.

This physical mumbo-jumbo and psychological analysis is all well and good, I hear you say, but surely the technical and tactical aspects of the game are more important?

Well, tactics perhaps less so, but being technically sound *is* the most important aspect. If you are not technically sound, you can only play to a particular level; you will always be inhibited. I would not say that the other aspects are made redundant – indeed, a good tactical approach may slightly ameliorate your technical weaknesses, but, ultimately, it is essential that you pay an exceptional amount of attention to the technical details of your delivery to ensure you can go to the next level.

Psychological aspects within the game will be scrutinized before tactical aspects in this book as I believe that it is harder to be psychologically prepared for a match than it is to learn the tactics of the game, which, by its very nature, is very much a subjective matter. Furthermore, tactical nous can sometimes come with experience. Although some have tried, I don't think a good tactical brain in bowls can really be learnt from a book. It is something you should be able to pick up yourself.

One thing I would quickly like to mention (so I don't bore you with the same information every time) is that when I talk of 'forehand' and 'backhand', this is for a right-handed player. If you are left-handed, obviously this will work the other way round.

Enjoy the book and, if you take one positive thing from it that you can practise on the green, then the journey will most definitely have been worthwhile.

Technical

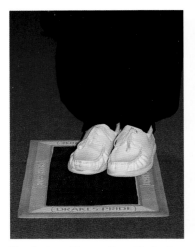

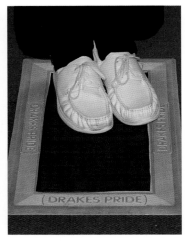

Your feet must be positioned in the line you want your bowl to travel.

This would be a typical position for someone bowling the backhand on an indoor surface. If you are tight/wide, you can alter your feet positioning accordingly with future deliveries.

1 Feet

Your hands are, first and foremost, of secondary concern. If your footwork is not correct, I am afraid to say you will be eternally hopeless at bowls. This is a fact. Of course, you may be able to get the occasional bowl close to the jack, but you will, more often than not, be lacking in any real accuracy.

I am sorry if you feel that you are too good a bowler to be bothered reading about positioning the feet. If you feel that way then skip a few pages. However, basic errors from even the most seasoned bowler can have catastrophic consequences, and I would urge you to keep reading, even if it is just for interest's sake.

Positioning of feet

Align your feet with the direction you want your bowl to go. Do not point your feet straight in line with the jack, unless the hand you are playing on draws straight up the middle. Don't point them too wide either – have *both* of your feet at the angle you want your bowl to travel.

If you don't do this, then this is when the problems start, as explained by Willie Wood:

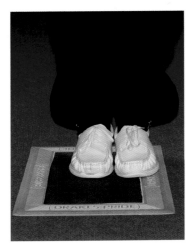

For a draw on an indoor surface, the feet are too straight here. This will mean the player has to overcompensate with the arm, and the delivery can lead to poor balance or looping, and most commonly bowling tight of the head.

Here, Willie Wood has spread his feet slightly apart but the main objective of pointing your feet in the direction of the line you need to take still prevails.

Once again, Willie has his feet apart, but they are both in the direction he wants to move forward. There is nothing wrong with this delivery whatsoever.

It is important that you point your feet in the line of delivery. Whether you are playing forehand or backhand, your right foot (if you are a right handed player), should be pointing up the line of delivery you are going to take.

You can do a number of things with your other foot. You can stand with both feet

Although this is an exaggerated picture showing Andy Thomson playing the forehand with feet positioned to play the backhand, it does highlight the awkwardness in your stance if your feet are not positioned properly.

The clinic stance is a good way of ensuring balance and consistency, as long as your feet are planted correctly (as shown).

No stance on the mat will be conducive to playing well if you don't point your feet correctly. On a draw, the front foot is far too straight here for an indoor green.

together or keep them slightly apart, as long as the other foot is telling the foot you put forward where it goes. It is the foot that is planted that tells the other one what direction you are playing.

If you fail to do this then you won't get your line consistently and many of your bowls will finish wide or narrow.

So, there you have it. Willie's description suggests that it is the foot you *don't* lunge forward that directs your foot that moves forward where to go. Of course, he is absolutely right. If the foot you plant is pointed incorrectly you will always have to over-adjust and this will inhibit you from finding an accurate line time after time.

I was once showing my delivery to a coach and he didn't know I played at all. He asked me: 'Why are you putting your feet together like that? You should always spread them slightly.' If I had been a new player then I wouldn't have had a clue what he was talking about, or why I should do that, and he wouldn't have had a logical answer if I had asked him. I felt like asking him: 'Why is it you can't get your bowls within four or five yards of the jack whereas I can?', but I very sensibly refrained.

What I am saying here is that I'm not even going to bother looking at how a coaching manual says you should or shouldn't do it. My analysis will be my own and, with input from some of the greatest players on earth, I feel it will be much more effective than any 'manual'.

I will not go into 'stance' until later in this section on technical play but one style adopted is known as the 'clinic' style, commonly used in South Africa. In this position, one foot is 'planted' forward and it is a 'static' delivery, designed to increase balance and simplicity. However, it is essential that you still keep to the fundamental principle of pointing your feet in the direction you want your bowl to travel. If you do this, you have grasped the most important and fundamental part that will get you on your way to playing better bowls.

2 Where to Look

I would love to be the omnipotent, omniscient guru of bowls with all the answers. However, I have to admit there is no specific right or wrong answer as to where you should look before and during your delivery, so I will write a list of ideas that you can try.

There is only one thing I would *not* do on the point of delivery (the split second when the bowl is released) – I would most certainly not look at the jack!

Willie Wood uses different techniques indoors and outdoors when looking at the point of delivery:

Outdoors, I will look for a little mark on the green. It might be a slightly different colour to the rest of the green – maybe brown or yellow or slightly greener.

I would take that little patch and hopefully that is the line. If it does materialize that it is near the line I want, I will be looking to bowl through that patch all the time for that end. However, if it is not exactly right, I can use it as a guide and play slightly inside or outside it.

When the mat is moved, I will look for a different patch on the green to use as a mark. Ideally, I would try and look for a patch about two-thirds of the way up the green where the bowl will begin to bend back.

Indoors, I look for the width of the rink. I *don't* look for the number on the rink next to me like many do. This makes no sense to me whatsoever. I take the green two-thirds of the way up the rink, so where the bowl will begin to arc back into the head.

I choose this method indoors because the carpet is all the same colour but outdoors I have the benefit of variable colours and patches to use as a guide.

So, even the best players have their own idiosyncrasies and ability to adapt to the conditions. 'Looking at the arc' and bowling through a patch on the green will both be explored in this chapter.

Looking at the jack

Unless you are playing on a straight outdoor surface, giving it no green what-soever, then *never* look at the jack at *your point of delivery*. If you look at the jack you are likely to bowl at the jack and see your bowl bend under the line time and time again. It is amazing how many times you see club bowlers bowling tight, far more commonly than wide, and in many cases this is a major contributing factor. My outdoor club swings well and you can play an

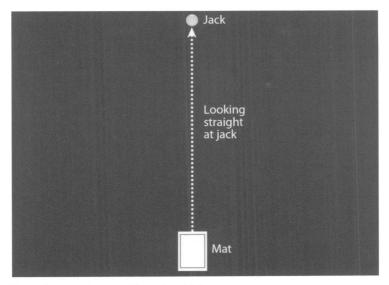

Do not focus on the jack at the point of delivery.

opponent from another club and watch him play the whole game tight, just because that is the green he will take at his home club.

On slower, straighter outdoor greens in the northern hemisphere, you may get away with bowling 'at' the jack as the 'straight' hand might literally be 'up the middle', but if you consistently play your games looking at the jack on point of delivery then you will really struggle for line and you will get caught out sooner rather than later.

Looking at an inanimate object on the bank or the ditch

This is a common way for bowlers to find a line. Usually this is done by looking at the rink marker indoors (David Gourlay is one player who likes to see the markers), and finding a line accordingly from that. This seems like a sensible approach to me.

David Bryant most commonly uses this when he plays. He uses the rink marker as a gauge and works from that:

I look at a pre-selected point of aim. Indoors, this is usually gauged by the rink mark. When you get on the mat, you play trial ends and you don't know anything about the green.

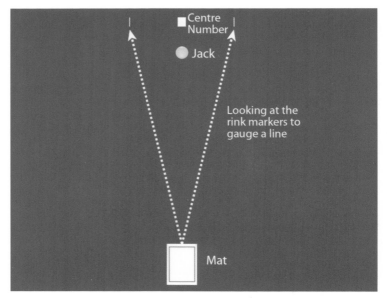

Looking at the rink marker is a common way for players to gauge the line.

When I get on a green in England I look at the boundary peg of the rink. I use those as a guide and work from there, depending on whether I am playing indoors or outdoors in the UK. Indoors it will usually be outside it; outdoors inside it.

David would occasionally change his style and look at something else, perhaps an advertising banner or something behind the rink, and gauge his line from that, but, as a club or county bowler, I wouldn't over-complicate matters, certainly not during a game, as you could end up playing even worse and confusing yourself.

In my opinion, unless you are a special player like David Bryant, looking for a guide beyond the bank over-complicates the matter, probably to the detriment of your game.

Objects bowlers will aim at regularly will include a scoreboard, a chair, accessibility steps or anything that they think is about the line they should be playing to.

You're also in trouble if you are aiming at something that could move, such as a chair, as you might find that the chair moves during a game, and

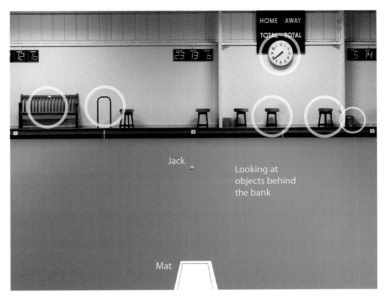

Looking at a chair or something behind the bank over-complicates matters.

then you have to find another marker to look for. Furthermore, by looking at something past the jack, you're not really gauging the length, and I think you are over-complicating a game that is complicated enough as it is already.

Indoors, I have also heard many people say they are looking at the rink number on the next rink, as Willie Wood mentioned. Unless you are playing with boomerangs and/or the indoor surface is exceptionally fast and swingy, I don't see how that can be any use, as if you bowl to it you will almost always be wide if the jack is on the centre of the rink.

I'm sorry, but I just don't see how looking at the centre marker on the next rink is an effective way to pick a line and length. I find it particularly bamboozling, and I do not know any 'world class' player who adopts this as a technique to find a line, yet many club-level bowlers insist on this as a way to gauge the line. If you use this technique, try another and see how you find it.

Looking at a patch on the rink

For outdoor bowls especially, there are always patches you can look to go over or just miss to the left/right to get the right line, as Willie Wood explained. I do not usually adopt this style but if the 'patch' is particularly prominent, I

If you're playing on rink four, there is absolutely no point looking at the centre marker on rinks three or five when playing the forehand or backhand draw. You will almost certainly bowl wide if you play to them.

will seek it out before delivery. For instance, I played in the national championships at Worthing and noticed there was a small divot where the sprinkler system was. I knew, with the mat back and the jack short, I had to be just inside this by approximately five to six inches. I used this to my advantage and ended up winning the game. I don't think my opponent noticed this line.

In this respect, you are guaranteed to find a good line if you consistently hit where you are aiming. Problems can arise outdoors if the rink changes through the course of the game or the mat is moved to a different position. If this happens, it is good if you can use another technique to adopt as a back-up, or find another patch. Indoors, this patch could be where there is a particular shade in the green reflecting from the light, or where a bit of dirt has coloured the carpet.

Looking a few yards in front of you

This is relatively similar to the previous idea in some respects, as you are picking a spot on the green to aim at.

Even if there is nothing to 'pick out' on the green, many bowlers find a patch where they want to bowl the bowl through - a particular blade of grass or piece of dust, dirt, etc.

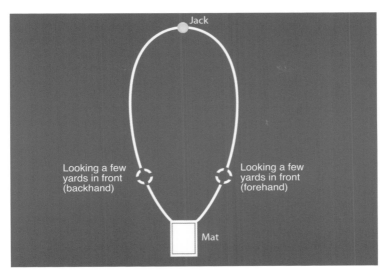

Looking a few yards in front to find an area you want your bowl to go through is a tried and trusted formula.

2010 World Bowls Tour singles champion Greg Harlow uses this technique to great effect and it is a good idea to employ this as your 'where to look'.

For this process, you must remember the jack length, so you have made a mental note of how long the jack is. This will, of course, mean you look at the jack and head and make a mental note of the length, preferably on numerous occasions. Your arm remembers the pace, not your eyes. However, I believe that a lack of concentration when using this technique could result in you getting the wrong weight, but that it is, in all likelihood, one of the best ways of getting the most consistent line. I don't use this technique as I would not trust myself to get the right pace time after time, but it is certainly something worth trying as a new way of finding a consistent line.

Looking at the ground in front of you

Taking the principle of looking a few yards in front to a new level, some (but not that many) bowlers do not look where they are bowling at all on point of delivery. They look at the ground right in front of them and deliver. Of course this is a ridiculous thing to do as you do not know where you are bowling to. Or is it such a stupid idea? One of the Australian greats, Ian Taylor, looked down on the floor just in front of him on the point of release. He had already got where

Ian Taylor looked at the ground right in front of him when he delivered, but I would suggest this is not something you should try.

the jack was mapped out in his mind. However, as a club bowler or someone trying to improve your game, I would dissuade you from this idiosyncrasy as Ian was a very special player. At club level, adopting such a technique could see drastically negative results, and leave you open to ridicule as people will quite rightly comment that you can't see where you're bowling to.

Not looking at anything in particular

Many players do not really have a specific area that they are looking to bowl into. Andy Thomson MBE explains:

> I don't pick a spot and bowl to it - I just get my line through my feet positioning, knowing where the jack is and then I look in the general area where I want the bowl to travel.

Tony Allcock also admits that he never really looked at anything in particular when he played, though he does state that people should look somewhere near the aiming point (where the bowl is going) and not the target point (jack) at the point of delivery. You could get away with looking at the target point to an extent outdoors on a tight hand but in other circumstances it will crucify you:

> When I taught people, explaining where to look was a very difficult element for me. If the truth be told, I didn't ever really know what I looked at.
>
> New Zealanders and Australians are far more disciplined. With these two countries, your aiming point and your target point are usually quite a distance away because of the pace and swing you use. They are looking at both and then look at the line before release.
>
> Outdoors in the UK and to an extent indoors, the aiming and target points are nearer together. Because of this, if you're a naturally gifted player and you are playing well, I would say you're probably not looking at anything.
>
> I would suggest trying to do what the Australians do. You are looking at the jack, then the aiming point, then the jack and then the aiming point again. You keep doing this and always release the bowl when you are looking at the aiming point.
>
> I think Ian Schuback [a great Australian bowler] did look at both [the jack and aiming point] and then release the bowl when looking at the aiming point.
>
> I taught people to look at the Australian way of where to look on point of release – certainly on the trial ends.
>
> People will pull bowls across because they forget that the aiming point and the target (the jack) are different.

By doing this, you are reaffirming the position of the target point in your mind and then casting your eyes over to the aiming point – where the bowl needs to go in order for it to ultimately finish next to the target point. If I'm being absolutely honest, this is the style I generally use as it works best for me and I think it is arguably the easiest way to gauge your line and length.

The aiming point, for Australians in general, is around the area where the bowls begins to 'arc', but it can also be any of the other aforementioned scenarios such as looking at a patch, etc. Looking at the arc is effectively what Willie Wood does indoors.

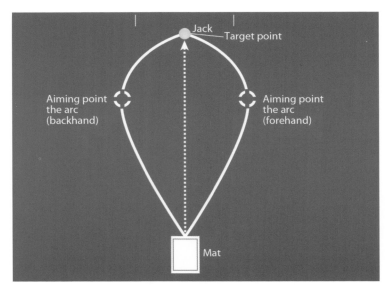

Flicking between the target and aiming point is a common strategy. If you are aiming for the arc, this is about where you will look indoors, depending on the rink.

Looking at the arc

When people say they 'look at the arc' they are looking at the widest point they are wanting the bowl to go to before it starts to hook back in. This lingo is no use to a bowler just starting out, but a bowler with some experience should understand what I mean by this. This is what Willie Wood does when playing indoors, which he mentioned at the start of the chapter.

Typically, this arc is approximately two-thirds of the way from the mat to the jack. Indoors, the green you take is more severe and so you will be looking wider, out somewhere near the width of the rink, whereas outdoors, more typically this may well only be a yard or two of width from the centre of the rink (or even tighter on some occasions). This style is a tried and trusted formula, and I would advocate that you try it when experimenting with where to look on your point of delivery. It is similar to the Australian style where you look at the green on point of release as, ultimately, you are looking at the same area, but more emphasis is placed on finding the line and pinpointing it before release, whereas the aforementioned Australian way is almost instantaneous and immediate after you look at the jack.

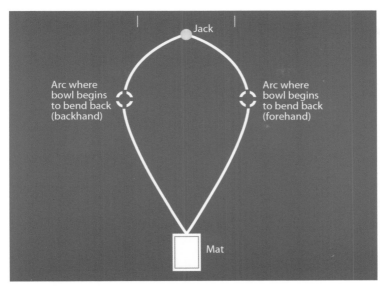

Looking at the arc is a good way to gauge the line. It will be somewhere around where the circles are for the backhand and forehand on a draw indoors.

Finally

Try all the strategies mentioned and see which one suits you. I would suggest you do this through practising thoroughly. See which one you feel is the most natural. As long as you don't look *at* the jack (or centre marker on the next rink) on point of delivery and you adopt one of the ideas in this chapter, you are not doing anything 'wrong' and I feel that it is about finding a style that gives you the most confidence that you will get the desired result with your bowl.

3 Grip

Before I go on to discuss the two major styles of grip, it is absolutely essential that you are playing with the correct-sized bowl. There have been plenty of old wives' tales expounded on this matter but I believe the best way to determine what size bowl is best for you is explained by Scottish international legend Willie Wood MBE:

If the wet bowl sticks to your hand like this, try the next size up. If the size up slips, then the one you could grip is the size for you.

You should wet your hands or the bowl, grip it how you would normally and then turn the bowl upside down. If it sticks without slipping then try the next size up. Once the bowl is too large to grip without it slipping out of your hand, the bowl is too large.

It is about using this process and finding a size that you feel comfortable playing with. Once you have done both of these, you should have the right size for you.

Claw grip

To use Andy Thomson as a point of reference, his grip is a perfect example of the 'claw grip'. He has the thumb very high on the bowl, rather than at the side of the wood.

This grip is the most popular one. You are holding the bowl with the tip of your fingers and 'stroking' the bowl away with your hand. Tony Allcock also

This side profile shown by Andy Thomson is a good example of a claw grip. You can see the gap from the thumb to the bowl.

used the claw grip when playing, believing it to be more beneficial than the cradle on faster surfaces:

The cradle grip is disadvantageous on a really fast outdoor or fast indoor green. With the claw grip, the fingers are at the top and there is a gap from the thumb to the bowl, which reduces strength. For the claw, the higher the bowl in the hand, the more the fingers come into play and the less the palm does. You can feel the bowl better in this way, but for a slow outdoor surface, the cradle is probably a more apt style of grip as you need to use your strength to reach the head.

The advantage of the claw grip is that you can get a good feel for the weight and feel the bowl come out of the hand smoothly. However, problems occur predominantly outdoors for bowlers who adopt this style of grip. In the northern hemisphere, and more specifically the UK, the weather is usually

This is how a claw grip would look from the front on.

Here, Willie Wood is showing his claw grip. Although adopting the same style of grip as Andy Thomson, there are subtle differences. Willie's thumb is lower on the bowl and his fingers are grasping more of the side of the bowl than Andy – he is 'gripping' the bowl more than Andy.

bad and, because of a crammed calendar, players have to play in the rain. In my opinion, it is difficult to grip with a claw style as it is more of a grip for finesse and perfection bowling; the bowl can easily just fall out of your hands on point of delivery if you are struggling to hold it for whatever reason (this can also include playing with the wrong size of wood). The way to attempt to ameliorate this is to apply a 'Grippo'-type substance – something that will stick to your bowl and allow you to have a better grasp, or just to dry the bowl thoroughly with a cloth.

Ironically, when the rain stops and the green dries up, the bowl can become *too* 'dry' and your fingers can once again slip when delivering. In this instance, you can either apply a sticky substance as previously mentioned, or wipe the bowl on the green to make it slightly damp and thus stick to the hand easier. Bowlers in continental Europe and the southern hemisphere very rarely have this problem.

Willie Wood explains that the claw is the type of grip used by the vast majority of top players, and he personally feels that it doesn't really have any disadvantages:

> I can't use the cradle grip and I have always used the claw. When I started playing we were still using wooden bowls and all wooden bowls are big bowls, which are hard to 'cradle', so I just used the claw grip and have kept using it for the rest of my career.
>
> I don't think there are any disadvantages with the claw grip really. You can get a good touch with it on the faster greens and most top-class bowlers will be using this style.

Willie disagreed with me about the fact that I believe the claw can be detrimental in wet weather, whereas Tony Allcock (who used the claw) agreed that it can be harder to grip with a claw style outdoors in the rain. It shows that it really is a matter open for debate. When two of the greatest-ever bowlers in Willie and Tony disagree, it shows that it is little more than personal opinion and there is no definitive right or wrong answer. However, on this instance, I'm in Tony's camp.

Cradle

The cradle grip is less common than the claw grip, but still used to good effect by players such as ex-England international Gary Smith.

The advantage of the cradle grip is that the bowl is sitting in the palm of your hand, so, in some respects, you are not 'gripping' it as such; you are palming it away on delivery. This means that you should not have the same problems with struggling to grip the bowl in wet conditions – you aren't really gripping it in the first place, you're 'pushing' it!

Unfortunately, it could be argued that you lose some of the 'feel' for the bowl, but, nevertheless, it is my personal grip of choice – but that is probably because I play the outdoor code at a more competitive level than the indoor.

In my opinion, it is also easier to get more power from this as the whole strength of your palm and hand can be used, which makes it ideal for a slow surface. Again, though, this is just my opinion, and once more my suggestion would be to try both grip styles indoors and outdoors and see which you feel most comfortable playing. It may be that the claw is suitable for indoors and the cradle for outdoors – don't be afraid to vary it.

This side-on picture clearly shows the difference in grip styles between the cradle and the claw.

This shot of the cradle grip shows that the bowler is cupping all of the bowl, with the thumb much lower.

4 Delivery: Keep it Tight (Including Looping)

Keep it compact!

If, on point of delivery, your arm and body are compact together, then there is little that can go wrong with the movement aspect of your delivery.

If you ever get the chance, watch England's Golden Boy Sam Tolchard. His delivery is very compact and his execution of every delivery is flawless. The exceptionally high backswing employed outdoors is an idiosyncrasy that Sam uses to great effect, but if you look at the compact nature of his delivery, you will see that his body is perfectly streamlined to where he wants his bowl to go.

Looping occurs when bowlers want to do the work for the bowl, rather than letting the bowl do it for itself. You must keep your body compact!

Sam Tolchard has a perfect delivery.

With his natural ability as well, it is not surprising that he is one of the best players around.

So, ultimately, keep your body tight, and even more importantly, keep your arm tight to your body on the point of delivery – let the positioning of your feet do all the work. Failure to do so will result in the commonly used and rarely successful style of 'looping'.

Looping

It's club bowlers' worst nightmare, but many of them do not even know they are doing it!

Fundamentally, looping occurs when you release the bowl away from your body. Think of cricket: you move your feet to the ball when batting and, if playing a straight drive or a defensive shot, then the feet and bat are as close as possible to be technically sound, and no

This practice should stop you from looping as you get tight to the wall and use your arm as a pendulum. If you try to loop, you'll hit your hand on the wall and soon remember not to do it again.

matter what the shot, the feet always move in whatever direction the player wants the ball to travel, just like in bowls.

The key is to let the bowl do the work, not your arm. If you do not, you will finish tight of the head, and then you will try to rectify this by releasing the bowl much earlier and getting it away horrifically badly and finishing wide and probably short.

If you loop, you lose. If this is a problem for you, really try to iron it out of your game and make sure your delivery is as compact as possible.

Willie Wood has an excellent technique for people to practise in order to stop any looping:

Looping gives you major problems, especially on the forehand. You are effectively trying to make a bowl bend from your arm, which is not a 'natural' delivery as *you* are trying to make the bowl bend, rather than letting it do it for itself. If you do this looping, you will probably go tight time and time again.

To stop looping, I suggest you find a wall, stand close to it and keep practising your delivery. This will stop you throwing your arm out as there is a wall in the way. By doing this, it should make your delivery more compact and stop your arm going too far away from your body.

5 Delivery: Running off the Mat

Paul Foster arguably 'runs off the mat'. In my opinion, Paul is the best bowler on the planet at the time of writing, and has been for a few years. This is certainly the case indoors, and possibly outdoors as well.

However, I am not saying that, in order to become a better bowler, you should run off the mat - quite the opposite in fact; I am just stating that the book on suitable deliveries can be torn up at times.

Like Paul, a lot of Scottish bowlers 'run off the mat'. One argument as to why they do this is because their outdoor surfaces are slower than anywhere else and it helps them to reach. I am sceptical about this as, from my experience of Scottish greens, they are generally faster, truer and better maintained than English ones.

However, top players who 'run off the mat' (Paul included) are not,

This shot actually shows that Paul does not run off the mat as such. At the point of delivery, his technique is flawless. Once he has delivered his bowl, his momentum pushes him forward and off the mat.

Running off the mat, as shown here (the player did not foot-fault on point of delivery), is not something I would advocate.

in my opinion, really doing so at all. Their deliveries are always identical time after time, and with the top players the bowl has already been delivered by the time the player has moved forwards off the mat.

Running off the mat does become an issue, however, when a player is not accustomed to doing it time after time. I admit my occasional guilt in this respect as, when the green gets heavier, I do tend to alter my delivery slightly to assist me in reaching the head. I do what I would like to call 'push' off the mat on particularly heavy outdoor greens where I have to reach, and whenever I play the drive. However, for drawing indoors, my feet will always remain firmly planted on the mat for a few seconds after I release the bowl.

'Pushing off the mat' outdoors works for me, but it can be problematical as you really do want to keep your delivery as consistent as you can possibly manage.

If you are keeping your feet on the mat half the time in a game and running off it the other half, then that is bound to be detrimental to your game, as consistency is key.

Running after a bowl

It can even be that a player has determined to run after his/her bowl no matter what, and this can often lead to the player spending more time thinking about immediately setting off after the bowl in an excitable manner than keeping focused on the finer details of delivery.

This happens especially at county games. There can be an expectation from team-mates that you would automatically run after a bowl, even more so when you are trying to save or make a big score. I fully advocate running after your bowl if you like it, but I would urge you to go through all the usual routines of your delivery before setting off. For instance, if you stay in delivery position for a couple of seconds as part of your usual delivery routine, then do this again before deciding to run after it.

Conclusion

I would generally suggest that you do not run off the mat, as will any manual telling you how to play the sport of bowls, but if it works for you then keep doing it – just make sure you are not foot-faulting. If your delivery is consistent and adheres to key technical aspects that are funda-mental to a good delivery, I don't think running off the mat will make that much difference.

There we have it: *a myth buster*!

6 Types of Delivery: Upright, Semi-upright, Semi-crouch, Crouch, Clinic

Stance and balance

With regard to stance, I suggest that it is important for you to choose the one that gives you the most balance, makes you feel most at ease and helps you get the bowl away the smoothest.

Regarding balance, it may not be your actual style of delivery *per se* that could be prohibiting you having a good balance on the mat, but what you are doing with your non-bowling hand.

If you are struggling to balance and you do not place your non-bowling hand on your knee, I would certainly suggest that it is worth giving it a try. This is a common practice employed by most bowlers where, for instance, if they are a right-hander, they will place their left hand on their left knee, and vice versa. This may well give you extra balance and help you to do something with your redundant hand.

Types of delivery

I would suggest that there are five major types of delivery – upright, semi-upright, semi-crouch, crouch and the clinic stance, the last being used most commonly in South Africa, which is a bowls 'giant'.

All of these styles have their benefits and occasionally their disadvantages. All are fine to use and I suggest that, if you want to improve your game, you should just try them all out when you practise. It's a case of trial and error.

Upright stance

This is when the starting position sees the player standing upright before delivery. Usually, the player will have the bowl in front of him/herself. Delivery will obviously involve bending down from this position. Because you are going quickly from a high position to a lower one, it is easy to misjudge your centre of gravity and you could find you are either bumping your bowl into the

This is an example of the upright stance.

Amy Gowshall is the most recognizable top player in today's game to use an upright stance.

ground or dropping it from a higher position than is ideal. If you use this type of delivery and are bumping your bowls into the ground, or not getting the bowl away smoothly, I suggest that you try a stance in which you are lower to the ground.

However, indoors, because the pace of your delivery will inevitably be slower, it is easier to stand upright and deliver your bowl without bumping it as you have more time to release it at the right moment.

To your advantage, with an upright stance, you can have a good position on the mat from which to view the head and, as long as your head movement is not too erratic, you should be able to be consistent in your delivery time after time.

The player I associate most with this stance in today's game is England star Amy Gowshall. The multi-world medallist stands up straight in her stance before delivery and is one of the best lady players on the planet. However, it is probably the trickiest delivery to implement successfully, particularly outdoors.

Semi-upright

This, along with the upright stance, is probably the most 'comfortable' position to adopt before delivery as it means you are not putting too much strain on your joints in the initial stance – though, inevitably, when you bend into your delivery, it does then put pressure on your joints.

This is arguably the most popular stance for bowlers and it suits many people well. However, you can struggle at times to get the bowl away, particularly as you get older, as Willie Wood explains in the semi-crouch delivery section.

Semi-crouch

I have defined this stance as the

The semi-upright stance.

semi-crouch and it is the delivery stance that I use. It puts some strain on the knees but I like the fact that I am close to the bowling surface without putting *too much* pressure on my joints and have my bowl close to the ground. In this respect, I feel there is less to go 'wrong'.

As Willie Wood states, it can be quite challenging having a higher position on the mat as age catches up on you and this can occasionally lead to mis-delivery, which is why he moved from the semi-upright to the semi-crouch delivery:

The semi-crouch position is a popular stance.

I used to use the semi-upright stance when I was younger and more athletic but, as I got older, I felt as though I was losing a bowl an end on delivery as you are further away from the delivery point on the green than if you were lower. I decided to stoop slightly, putting a slight bend on my legs so that I would be closer to the green. This seems to work much better for me nowadays. With the semi-upright stance, I wasn't grounding the bowl properly for about one delivery in every four and you lose your weight with that. It would bounce and/or wobble on the point of delivery.

When you lose a bowl out of four you are going to struggle and you can't play against the top players with three bowls – you need every one.

I get my bowl away much smoother now I use the semi-crouch. There are no disadvantages to this type of delivery – you can draw or play the drive and anything in between with absolutely no problem.

I would advocate to most bowlers to use this type of delivery. It has worked for me and I know a whole load of other bowlers who have been successful with that style – Alex Marshall being one of them! We have a similar delivery style – both of us are slightly stooped and our knees bent and we both put our hand on the knee.

The crouch delivery.

Robert Weale is the most successful exponent of this style at the moment.

Crouch

Welshman Robert Weale is the most successful exponent of this type of stance in today's game. It is a perfectly fine way to position yourself before delivery, but puts a great deal of stress on your knees and thus, in this respect, is not a 'lasting' delivery. David Bryant would always use a crouch but come upright on a slower surface, whereas on a faster surface, he would deliver from the crouch stance. However, as age has caught up with him, he cannot use this style any more. However, it is a perfectly good stance as long as it does not strain your knees too much.

The positive aspect of this style of delivery is your low centre of gravity. Because of this, there is very

David Bryant used to use the crouch for faster surfaces so that he was lower to the ground and could just touch the bowl away. He would rise up from the crouch, but to a lesser extent on the faster surfaces.

little to go wrong. Your body movement is minimal with this style as
you have to do less; you crouch and
deliver, and it is perfect for faster
surfaces.

Clinic

For the clinic stance, the position you
take is 'fixed' as you put your front
foot forward (obviously, your left
foot if you are right-handed, or your
right foot if you are left-handed).

Using this delivery means that
there is less to think about and go
wrong - you are not moving your feet
and your arm is just acting as a
pendulum.

The clinic stance is popular in South
Africa.

I would suggest that this could be problematical if you struggle to reach
on heavy outdoor surfaces, as all of your strength has to be in your arms
because you cannot use your feet and forward movement to add momentum
in the delivery of your bowl.

However, I cannot foresee any problem in using this stance indoors. Doing
so will ensure that your feet and body are positioned correctly and that there
is very little to think about apart from the swing of your arm.

Willie Wood is a strong advocate of this type of delivery and does not see
any problems with reaching the head with this type of stance, which is slightly
at odds with my own opinion, as just stated. Willie says:

This is mainly a South African stance. They adopted the stance many
years ago. I went to South Africa in the 1970s and they were using it
then and they are still using it now. Gerry Baker - one of South Africa's
best known players - uses it.

The advantages of this stance are that you have a good, stable
balance and the delivery is quite simple. It is a good and lasting
delivery.

Personally, I don't think there are any disadvantages with it.

There are one or two top bowlers who use the clinic stance in the

UK. Iain McLean, who has won the Scottish singles indoors and out, uses it, but it is not a commonly used stance.

Perhaps it doesn't go into the coaching manual in the UK? I really don't know why so few people use it.

It is a perfectly good stance to use and allows you to focus fully on the pendulum action of your arm when delivering, taking away the added worry of moving and positioning your feet correctly during delivery.

7 Delivery: Differences for Indoors and Outdoors

If the green is faster, your delivery should be slower and lower. If the green is, putting it bluntly, as slow as hell, your backswing and delivery should be faster and you could also start your delivery from a higher, semi-upright or upright delivery, as detailed in the previous chapter. This should help you with momentum but, at the same time, you should try to avoid making drastic changes to your delivery. It's a balancing act you must perform yourself.

Adapting your stance

While I would not usually advocate that you adapt your stance depending on the pace of the surface, this ploy can be used to good effect if you have the ability to alter your stance whilst ensuring it doesn't detrimentally affect your delivery.

As detailed in the previous chapter, David Bryant would adapt his stance. He would always start in the crouch delivery for all surfaces but, when playing on a heavy green, he would then come up, take a large stride and get his bodyweight behind to reach. For a fast surface, he would stay low, keep his backswing to a minimum and 'stroke' the bowl away:

> If you're on a heavy green, you need to make the most of your height and length of backswing and length of step.
>
> If you play in Australia or New Zealand on the ultra-fast greens, the closer you can get to the ground, the better.
>
> Basically, on a fast green, you don't want a lot of bodyweight over the bowl which we have to use outdoors in the UK. We have to use a long step and a long backswing and stand reasonably high to get the power to get up the green.

On fast surfaces, it isn't about having the power to get up the green – you're keeping your power back.

Whenever I practised on a fast green after being in the UK, the bowl never left my sight as my backswing was so little.

Once the bowl has gone past your back leg, you can't see how far it has gone back. What you need is a shorter backswing, a shorter step and to be closer to the ground, so you are more or less 'stroking' the bowl up the green.

For a slow surface, I used to get in the crouch for my delivery, but then I would come completely upright and I would take a long step and get all my bodyweight over the bowl.

I would use the crouch and stay in that position indoors and on fast outdoor surfaces.

This makes perfect sense, and, although not to such a drastic extent as David, I believe most of us do adapt our stance and delivery according to the conditions we are playing in.

Have you ever noticed when you go back indoors for the first time that the green seems impossibly fast, but after a few games you have adapted to the pace? You may even berate the green for being too slow after a few matches. That is because you have made subtle, perhaps even subconscious, changes to your delivery. You will have most certainly slowed your delivery down, your backswing will not be as vicious and you are probably getting slightly lower during your stance as well, perhaps without you even knowing it. We all adapt to survive, and making these changes shows your initiative and the initiative of the human mind to adapt accordingly.

8 Playing a Runner

How to play a runner?

Technically, this shot comes into blurred territory, and, to me, a runner can be anything from two yards of pace to ten yards of pace.

Technically preparing for a shot which requires two yards of pace is unequivocally different from playing with ten yards of pace, especially indoors.

Use your brain, take your time and concentrate. If you do all that this

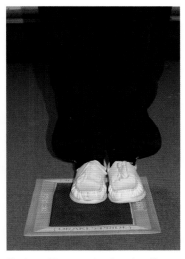

Positioning your feet more centrally is the first thing you need to do, but make sure you don't overcompensate.

Playing with a couple of yards will require a fair amount of green (particularly indoors). Make sure your feet are not too straight, as shown here. Your arm and body will need to overcompensate otherwise.

chapter tells you to, there is a chance you'll get the required result at the end of it.

To reach with the required amount, you can increase the height and speed of your backswing to increase the pace of the bowl and reach the head with the required weight.

Runner indoors

The most important thing to stress is that your feet should be positioned where you want the bowl to travel. Obviously, the more pace you add to your delivery, the tighter your line will be, and the positioning of your feet should work accordingly with this. The faster the pace of the bowl, the more central-ized your feet should be pointing.

If you are literally playing just two yards, you should not change anything that you would do normally, save for looking at how much less line you judge you need and pointing your feet ever so slightly more centrally, and adding the required weight.

This process should be used all the time, so if you plan to add another five yards of pace with your next delivery you just alter your positioning on the mat accordingly as you will inevitably take a finer line. However, your delivery model should remain the same so that you keep to a routine and less can go wrong.

It sounds simple but it is incredible how often people do not adjust at all and then simply say 'it's hanging out'. It's 'hanging out' because they have added a considerable amount of pace and have not adjusted their line proportionally. We all know that there is an amazingly long excuse book for bowlers, and it is important that you don't fall into the trap of tricking yourself that the rink is conspiring against you.

Runner outdoors

Lines vary considerably outdoors and so it is very difficult to suggest how to play a 'running shot'.

More often than not (a lot more often in the UK), an outdoor surface will take a much tighter line than an indoor one. Even if you have a model of bowl that swings an exceptional amount for the outdoor game, and a 'large marble', which takes very little bias for the indoor game, your bowl outdoors will require less green on the whole.

Thus, to this end, and as always the first point of reference, it is essential that you check your feet. You do everything the same as if you are doing it indoors, but the positioning of your feet is likely to be less exaggerated. For instance, some outdoor surfaces may take a line straight up the middle. In this instance, there isn't a great deal you can do with your feet, apart from pointing them straight up the rink for a draw, runner or drive.

For straighter outdoor greens, it may well be that, for a runner, you have to have your feet pretty much straight, as shown here.

However, the vast majority of outdoor surfaces will take some green and thus you 'shave' the angle of your feet according to the pace and line you wish to implement.

Final tip: always remember that you are working in harmony with your feet. Don't you *dare* think about looping!

9 Firing

If you get too near the jack, you invariably pay for it. If your opponent(s) get(s) too close, they deserve to see their good work go to burn and, more than likely, your choice of shot to make your opponents rue getting so close is the drive shot (or it should be).

I believe the best way to demoralize your opponent(s) is by using the draw shot effectively and taking all of their count out by getting nearest to the jack that way. However, there will be instances where the draw shot is not the percentage shot and the drive is the most sensible option to play. We will explore 'percentages' later in the book (see Chapter 24).

Driving successfully

Compaction is key – keep your delivery as you would normally and make sure your feet are pointed in the line you wish your bowl to travel.

Don't think 'I can't do that' and, if you usually just play lead but find yourself driving, don't assume you will miss – you should have practised the drive anyway to improve your general development.

Furthermore, if you are driving and you plan to get your excuse book out – don't bother! It's of no help to your team-mates. Just try your best and if you miss by a distance then you can always say sorry; no one has died (unless you really did miss by a long way)!

Furthermore, if the drive is the only shot available and you are rubbish at it, don't try to convince your team-mates that you should be drawing. You could make the head worse. It may be better if you just throw your bowl in the gutter and let the player after you drive with greater accuracy.

David Bryant strongly believes that, to drive accurately, you draw your arm back slowly and then, when your arm comes to its highest point, bring the arm and bowl down with great speed. Usually, when most players drive, the whole action is sped up, including taking your arm back high with the bowl, but David believes this can be detrimental to your delivery of the bowl:

This is an important part with the drive: when your arm comes back, it comes back slowly! You line yourself up; you are looking at the point of aim. Your arm comes right back as far as it can, but slowly, and then your movement from there is very fast. If your whole delivery is fast, including drawing the bowl behind you, you will struggle to keep the movement fluent and your delivery may become messy.

I think that's something definitely worth a try and should ensure that your delivery model is kept consistent.

Driving too wide

If you find you are driving too wide, the first thing I suggest you should do is check where you are pointing your feet. It may be that you haven't adjusted your feet from the drawing line and that you are not angled correctly.

If your feet aren't positioned correctly and are pointed out far too wide, the only way that you will hit the head accurately is by bringing the bowl across your body, which is something you definitely do not want to get into the habit of, as your bowl could go anywhere.

This would be a good starting position for a drive on the backhand.

This would be a good starting position for a drive on the forehand.

It is important that your swing is tight to your body and that your timing is correct.

Driving too tight

The most common reason for firing *very* tight is the fact that you will be pulling the bowl across your body. If your excitement at playing the drive and desire to obliterate the head finds you consistently missing tight of the head, you are doing too much and overcompensating.

If you are struggling with the drive, let your local coach try to help you. If you are finding you aren't getting anywhere with that, have a word with the best player in your club and see if he/she will help. It may be that you are just making a simple, tiny mistake that can make all the difference.

Remember, when you are playing the drive, you should be keeping an identical delivery model to a draw shot, though inevitably the action will have to be faster and the backswing higher.

10 Wobbling a Drive

Wobble, wobble, wobble! Roll up, roll up - where will the bowls go? Pin the bowl on the donkey?

Unless the wobble is manageable - which in the vast majority of cases it isn't - you don't really know where the bowl is going to veer off to when driving.

It is commonplace that bowlers, when they elect to drive, have a problem with 'controlling' the bowl.

The first thing I would suggest is to look at how you hold your bowl. Are you holding it exactly as you would if you were drawing? It is important you check your fingers are where they usually would be.

Swing

Is your backswing similar? I'm not saying *the same*, as it will inevitably be higher and faster than it would be for a draw so you can generate the required extra pace, but it is important that it is consistent with your delivery model and that you are not snatching or mistiming the release of the delivery.

Timing is important - release the bowl too soon and it will probably just miss and hit the ground hard and wobble; release it too late and it will go up in the air and bounce and thud on the surface. This will also heighten the chance of the bowl wobbling up the green. If you're struggling with the timing on your release, then I would suggest that the answer is to practise, practise, practise. You'll know when your timing is right as you should get the bowl away well; everything should feel right and if you are adhering to basic technical principles then it should be close to hitting the head.

There is nothing wrong with practising for hours, solely electing to choose the drive. People may sneer, snigger and claim that you're damaging the bank, but if you want to improve in every area, you must practise everything, especially your weaknesses.

Body

Is your body all moving in the right direction, or is the thought of throwing a bowl down as fast as humanly possible a prospect that you find so exciting that all technique goes out of the window?

If you find, when you fire, that your delivery is not as it would be for any other delivery, and this is proving detrimental to your performance when playing the drive, my advice is simple: play with less pace. It is obvious that you are trying to hit it too hard. Indoors especially, you don't need to exert every bit of your strength when driving – it's the old adage of quality, not quantity.

After these pointers, I have to admit I don't adhere to all of them when playing the full-out drive – I run off the mat to gain speed and thus do not keep it exactly consistent, but it seems to work for me. (I wouldn't try it if I were you, though.)

If you hit six heads out of ten with fifteen yards of pace, or four heads out of ten with a full-out drive, it is better to play with fifteen yards of weight. Although it is exciting to play the full-out drive (and when it works well it looks explosive), if you are missing the head too often then play with less pace and see if it increases your accuracy.

Psychology

11 Introduction to Psychological Approaches

I believe that psychology in the sport of bowls is so important that I have decided to put it in earlier than tactical approaches. Over a certain period, your tactical nous should hopefully be accrued from learning from others and seeing what works well for yourself. Psychologically speaking, though, you can continue to make the same mistakes again and again and always be inhibited by your own shortfalls in this usually neglected area within the sport.

Pessimism is rife in bowls. 'You won't get that', 'You're playing the wrong hand' – comments like these are evidently detrimental to a team performance, yet we are all (or nearly all of us) guilty of it.

That is bad enough, but then, when added to the mix is the good luck their opponents are getting and conversely the bad luck they themselves are having, bowlers go into a whole new depth of negative talk and a profound state of 'feeling sorry for themselves'. Thinking like this will not only make your performance worse; it will enhance your opponents' game as they chuckle at your misfortune.

John McGuinness plays bowls for England and appreciates the importance of psychology in bowls.

This section will scrutinize how to prepare for a game, how to play in a particular position, and how to overcome any psychological issues when you meet the players who always beat you. Furthermore, I will also look at the kind of mindset you need to get the psychological advantage over your opponents.

Psychology goes far deeper than being purely about the mindset you should be in to play as well as you can. It is also imperative that you consider strongly how to be a positive influence on the rink, and how you approach discussions and help your team-mates, which can positively influence the entire rink to perform better.

Thus, in addition to addressing

Professor Ian Maynard worked with the England Commonwealth Games squads in 2002 and 2006.

how your psychological approaches can help you improve your own perform-ance, this chapter also focuses on simple but effective techniques to help you get the most out of your team-mates.

In the article reproduced here, John McGuinness, Performance Co-ordi-nator for the 2006 England Commonwealth Games team in Melbourne and an England international in his own right, explains the impact the work of sports psychologist Ian Maynard made on the England Games team, and how psychology can help bowlers in general:

The use of psychology in bowls

I introduced Ian into the support team as part of the preparations for this prestigious event in the bowls calendar. If the truth be known, with such a talented and seasoned bunch of players, I was somewhat apprehensive about how the 'psychology' element was going to be received by my players, particularly given that they all naturally applied strong psychology in their game anyhow, often without realizing that they were doing it. It was one of the reasons why they were all so successful in the first place.

In my experience, performance enhancement strategies and techniques only work if everybody is committed to it, understands and appreciates its value and is dedicated to implementing the practices and techniques that work best for them. This is not an easy thing to achieve and indeed there is a level of psychology required to ensure that players see and understand the benefits that this complex discipline can deliver to their game.

I, together with my magnificent team managers, John Bell and Mary Price, needed no convincing of how important it was and, looking back now, I wish we had more time to do more work with Ian in this area. I knew how critical the psychological mindset was, particularly as the Melbourne Games was the first one to introduce the sets play format, which included a two bowl pairs format (thankfully, something that has since been modified). Whilst many of the players were familiar with sets play format through their involvement in various professional indoor events, it was mainly in singles play and not as part of a team and in a round robin format such as that employed at the Games.

Ian's involvement proved invaluable, particularly as he was able to bridge the gap between theory and application and how sports psychology would specifically apply to our sport. One of Ian's key focuses was on helping players deal with the psychological impact that tie-breaks would create. It was inevitable that there would be a significant number of games decided in this way.

There is no doubt in my mind that Ian's involvement proved invaluable to that particular England team competing in Melbourne. He had a pleasant and refined way of getting across some key strategies, without making it look too theoretical or unrelated to bowls.

As a more general statement, I don't think there is anybody who plays our great sport that has never said on at least one occasion to a colleague, 'Ahhh – sure, it's just all in your head'. It may be related to choosing a set of bowls or to playing a certain opponent or even perhaps to playing on a certain rink number or getting to a particular score in a game. Regardless of what it is, what goes on

*in our head, before, during and after we play has a significant influ-
ence on how we perform and, at the highest level, can often be the
difference between success and failure. In my opinion, nearly all of
our most successful bowlers in the past and indeed present day
demonstrate significant psychological strength and in particular
real mental toughness in their game. Quite often this has been
without actually realizing that they are applying 'psychology'. It's
just something that they do naturally. The desire to build on this
and continue to strive for new levels of performance is what differ-
entiates mediocrity from greatness for those that have the inbuilt
ability and talent.*

John's insight into the importance of psychology at the highest level of the
game does not mean that psychology is something that cannot be applied by
all bowlers. Quite the opposite, in fact, as John states that we all use
psychology in some way or other before, during and after a match, which
chimes very well with the following chapters.

Tony Allcock worked with Ian Maynard four years earlier for the 2002
Commonwealth Games in Manchester when he held the position of Performance Co-ordinator, and stressed that psychology is as much about knowing
yourself as anything else:

> This was a new thing for bowls. People marvelled at the idea that a
> bowler should need any psychological assistance at any level.
>
> After working with him, I found that bowls is more about
> psychology than anything else. It is about reading the opposition and
> the knowledge of oneself. You usually think it is the opposition that
> you have to overcome but you must know yourself first ... then your
> team-mates and then you can consider your opponents. Success
> comes from within.

This section will explore how you can apply certain psychological techniques
to aid your game and get you to 'know yourself'. When I scrutinize how to be
psychologically prepared as lead, two, three and skip, I have also added the
'practicalities' of the position as the two issues can become inextricably
combined at times, and this also gets the practical side of the position out of
the way so that I can explore different avenues later in the book.

12 Preparation Before a Match

Bowls is played almost exclusively by amateurs. There are very few elite players who ply their profession in bowls, and many players of working age inevitably have to rush off after work and run onto the green to start the match as soon as they get there.

This is the way of the world, I am afraid, but, if you are fortunate enough to get fifteen minutes to prepare for a game, no matter how serious the game may be, then make the most of it.

Preparation is not something that you can just research and assume that what you read will be right for you. Just taking in a few moments of peace and quiet can potentially make the world of difference, ensuring you start the match in the correct frame of mind.

Everyone should prepare in one way or another and have routines in place so that their preparation comes naturally. At elite level, this preparation starts months and weeks beforehand, but at other levels it may be that you need a routine ready when you get to the club fifteen minutes before the start, as Ian Maynard explains:

> The bowls match does not start when you step onto the green. You would have your fifteen-minute warm-up. It doesn't always have to be an hour or longer.
>
> If you are running late, you have to pull out the most important elements and that is why I would encourage people to have three routines before the game – one is ten to fifteen minutes, one is the hour (which you will hopefully use 99% of the time) and one perhaps of three hours. Obviously, if you work, the last two could be impossible.

So, whether it is regarding your delivery or your preparation, you must have a routine and keep to it. This familiarity will mean you have less to think about as you consistently do the same thing time and time again, until it becomes second nature.

Take your time

So, it's 6.10 p.m. and you have rushed to get to the club for a 6.15 p.m. start. It may be that you have just finished work, or that you were stuck in traffic, or that you fell asleep on the couch. It really doesn't matter what you have been doing; you still have time to get yourself in the right state of mind before you play.

You know what your opponent's response will be: 'What time do you call this?' 'I've been waiting here for half an hour already.' 'You're always late.' 'Come on, let's get on with it.' All four of these utterances, unless clearly meant in jest, are designed to unsettle you and you should make sure you ignore the jibe. Good for them that they've had time to spare; maybe they should have spent their time more wisely rather than spending most of it getting irritated by your non-arrival. I'm not advocating telling them where to put their watch, or being rude to them in reply; I think you can make a short apology and say you will be with them shortly.

Now you have these few minutes to spare, use them wisely. If you need the toilet, go to the toilet; if you like to sit down in the changing rooms for two or three minutes before you start a match, do that.

The main point I would like to make is *do not be rushed*. Only when you finally feel ready (within reason) to engage in a three-hour bowls match should you go out on to the green.

It is up to you what you do with your 'spare' time before a match commences. There are a number of things that you *can* do and it really is about doing whatever suits *your* needs!

Distractions

If you occupy a position in the club such as captain and you know that arriving early for a match will only mean that people nag you about your selection choices, or that they don't like playing in this position and with that person, then stay in the car or in the toilet and compose yourself for as long as you need before turning up a few minutes beforehand to play your match. Don't get there an hour early, satisfy everyone else's needs and play a rubbish game because your mind is on everything else but the match.

I admit I am being a hypocrite here and that I should listen to my own advice at times, but you should always think about *your* needs; you would do in any other sport.

Talking (or not) to others

I like to have a chat with people before the game commences. I feel it relaxes me and takes me away from whatever I may have been doing prior to turning up to play.

Some sports psychologists may find this approach rather suspect and not befitting any typical approach prior to a match, but, first and foremost, I enjoy bowls because it is a sociable sport, and camaraderie and good manners should always prevail – and I also think it helps me to relax.

Even for a competitive match, I still like to talk to people and smile and share a joke. It is what I am accustomed to doing and it is how I enjoy playing and relaxing. Once I prepare to step onto the mat I am completely focused and the only thought on my mind is the shot I am about to play and get!

If you share my approach, you should be aware that there is a good chance that your opponent may not be as talkative as you, and this may be because he/she has to focus by engaging in minimal human interaction. Talking is seen by many as a distraction that leads to a lack of concentration and poor performance and, even though I disagree from my own perspective, I admit that I may not be quite so talkative at a really competitive tie.

If you find that talking does distract you from the game you are about to play and thus has a negative impact, then don't do it. It's not rocket science – it is just a matter of testing the water and seeing what is right for you. However, if your wish is for peace and quiet, it is important that you remain pleasant and polite to those who try to engage you in conversation and don't use the excuse that you are concentrating to be abrasive to others.

Getting 'in the zone'

Ten minutes to yourself can provide the solace required to get 'into the zone'. If you've never really thought about preparing yourself before the start of the game, try to spend a few minutes in your own company – you never know, it may focus you better for the start of the match and you can hit the ground running. I would try new things and ways of preparation before a less important fixture first, though; a wholesale change in preparation before an important match may not be wise.

'Getting in the zone' is something that we try to do in every sport. In team games such as football and rugby, we will have a team-talk from the manager or the captain of a team. In bowls, this is rarely done, and rinks of players can go onto the green for the first time without even knowing the names of those with whom they are playing.

It would be a culture shock for bowlers if the skip of the rink quickly summoned his/her players to have a get-together and team-talk, but there is no reason why you shouldn't all have a chat with your team to set out expectations and tactics and scrutinize your opposition.

Let's get physical

Physical exercise can also be of benefit. I will not go into depth in this chapter as to which stretches may be of use, as that information is covered in Section Five of the book, but suffice it to say a gentle warm-up may not only make you feel more supple, but also give you peace of mind and a small chunk of time to reflect on the forthcoming game before you commence battle.

13 Psychological Issues During a Match

Rain during (and before) a match

Let's start with God's tap. Outdoors, particularly in the UK, rain can be a massive factor and many a time players and teams will be sitting around waiting. In this respect, it is important that you adapt your routine and are ready in the eventuality that rain delays play, as made abundantly clear by Ian Maynard:

> Typically, in the UK, it is raining, and you may have to adapt your preparation to tailor it to the weather and delayed starts. The delays in the game are often when you sit there worrying and getting anxious so you must have some sort of activity there to help you occupy your mind.

Of course, if you are taken off the green because of rain, you need to occupy your time productively and not worry about whether you will be able to get back out or not. This can be detrimental to concentration.

As Tony Allcock explains, Ian Maynard focused heavily in his work with the 2002 Commonwealth Games team on 'controlling the controllable'. Rain does not come under this remit:

> Ian made it clear that you can only control the controllable. When it rains, for instance, you could sit and read a book, eat a banana, sit in the car or occupy the time however it will help you most.

What you don't do is sit there and bite your nails, look at the clouds, hoping it stops.

Now that the issue of rain is out of the way, let's look at some of the more obvious problems that can arise during a game.

Bad start

If you've prepared according to what suits you best and you still endure a nightmare start, don't panic! It may just be that you have not had the 'rub' of the green (although don't use this as an excuse) or are just struggling to find the green and your game – these things happen!

Before we delve into the finer psychological details of how to rectify this nightmare start, you may just want to check the more obvious potential issues. For example, are you playing the 'correct' hand? For outdoor bowls, I would usually consider this to be the more 'giving' hand, where if you bowl slightly wider or tighter than you intended, it will not punish you as much. For indoors, it will be the hand that does not 'track', or that you feel most comfortable on. If you are leading, I would usually suggest playing down one side of the rink – backhand up, forehand back, unless you feel the rink plays better backhand and backhand or forehand and forehand.

However, if you feel you are playing the correct hand and you are doing everything you should have been and are still struggling, you must get in the right frame of mind to play better and hope that the score reflects this.

Blaming the rink, your opponent's 'narrow bowls', the sun in your eyes or the lighting if you are playing indoors will not help you. Poor sportsmen make poor excuses; good sportsmen do something about it!

When on the mat, you must not be thinking about all the ends that have passed. If these play on your mind, you will continue to play badly. If you are in a team game, your team-mates will be doing one of two things: either they will be trying to encourage you or they will be niggling at you. Hopefully they are doing the former but don't just feel sorry for yourself – do something about it.

When on the mat, focus entirely on the bowl you are about to bowl. Just try to get close to the jack, or play whatever shot you are attempting to execute. In this situation, I wouldn't necessarily be telling myself that now is the time to start playing well, as this could create undue pressure and have the opposite effect to that desired.

The result is only a concern when the game is over. Your focus should be on playing better and getting in the right psychological mindset to make some kind of challenge for your opponent(s).

Keeping momentum

You're 20–2 up, you're relaxed – life is good and you feel invincible. Before you know it your opponents have regrouped, improved, won the end and changed the jack length and your casualness has resulted in a downward spiral as you now struggle with your weight and line and you are put under pressure end after end. Before you know it, your opponents are back in the game.

How do you rectify this? First, never feel sorry for your opponents! This attitude can be slightly moderated in friendly matches as no one wants an overenthusiastic rink relishing the summary execution of the opposition, but certainly, in all competitive play, you are only ever one end away from disaster, which can have far more serious consequences for the rest of the game, and, psychologically speaking, even for the rest of the season!

I would advise you to play every end with the same focus, attention and drive that you have applied to every previous end.

In team games, I think a five-shot lead is always a make-or-break moment. I usually skip and I will always tell my rink at this stage that we must not relax and let up, but must keep pushing. A 10–5 score is close, but if you score another five shots without reply, 15–5 may feel insurmountable to your opponents. Instead of looking to recover the deficit, they may well adopt a damage limitation tactic and this could be a positive scenario for you.

Relaxation (or, more specifically, complacent relaxation) is something that you should not feel in competitive play and I would seriously steer away from it in matchplay. Now, this is something that needs qualifying. It is important that you feel relaxed in your rink; it is imperative that you communicate well together and feel relaxed in each other's company. As an aside, there is nothing worse than a dispute in shot selection, resulting in the player feeling that if he/she goes against the advice of team-mates, then they will almost be willing the player on the mat to fail. It is essential that, at the time of playing the bowl, everyone is on the same wavelength and all are fully behind the shot played and the player playing it. Psychologically speaking, this will put the player of the bowl at ease so he/she doesn't have to worry about upsetting people and can purely focus on the job in hand – executing the shot to be played.

Fundamentally, if you are playing well, you must keep to the same technical routine you have been doing to ensure that you, either as an individual, or as a team, keep totally focused and don't let up. Feel relaxed as a team but don't get complacent and lose concentration.

Finishing off a game

This is the nitty-gritty – it sorts out the men from the boys, and the women from the girls. You may get away with playing like a hero for two-thirds of a game to achieve the required result sometimes, but eventually there will come a time when you will need to finish off a game.

Consistency in everything you do in bowls is key, whether in your delivery, your approach to a game or any idiosyncrasies you perform that make you feel at ease.

If you were focused before, you must now be super-focused, but do not put too much stress and pressure on yourself. Don't think about the outcome of the game too much; that will be determined on the last end in team matches or when someone hits 21 in singles; just concentrate on playing the shot you are electing to play, keep your delivery model consistent and play your bowl.

It is possibly even more important at this stage of the game to think: 'I will get the shot!' That will help give you the confidence to go and get it. However, what is far more important is that, when you get this shot, you must be psychologically prepared for your opponent to take it back off you.

If you are ready for your opponent to get a shot back, even if it looks nigh-on impossible, it will, at worst, mean you are ready and prepared to play your next shot and at best you will be pleasantly surprised if your opponent misses.

Controlling nerves/stress

If you do get nervous when playing a game of bowls, then my suggestion is ... don't! Ultimately, no one is going to die and the world will not end, though it can feel like that sometimes.

However, that is not to say that you should approach the last few ends nonchalantly.

Seriously, I believe that if you are getting in a panic then you should do some deep breathing. It could make a difference and calm you down a bit. However, I wouldn't do this in the company of others or they may think something could be wrong or that you are odd.

Thirty seconds to yourself could also make a difference. I would never advocate disappearing in a singles game unless you need some water or the toilet, as I find it exceptionally bad etiquette and would never do that myself, but if you are in a team game and feel that a few seconds to yourself will help, then take those few seconds to go somewhere else, stand off the bank, close your eyes or whatever else you may need to do to compose yourself. Once again, I would suggest you do this away from the sight of your opponents as they may see that you are nervous and exploit that weakness.

By the same token, don't tell your opponents you are nervous or that you have not played many competitive matches before – yes, it may possibly lull them into a false sense of security, but it will more than likely spur them on.

There are psychological ways of controlling your nerves, and stress can be dissected into two areas – physical (somatic) and in your head (cognitive). Ian Maynard explains how these issues can be rectified:

Fundamentally, there are two types of anxiety: cognitive and somatic anxiety.

Cognition is about the mind and around negative thoughts – so you have to look how to turn negative thoughts into positive ones with cognitive restructuring and rationalization. Sometimes, processing words that bring you back into your delivery mode can help you over-come that.

Somatic anxiety relates to the symptoms of stress. This could be sweaty hands or a racing heart. This is the physical side of anxiety. For this, you need a physical solution, which usually revolves around breathing techniques.

Ultimately, you have to identify which anxiety you have (some-times it is both) and practise a solution to these problems.

The first time you have a negative thought, it could take you ten minutes to come up with a solution for that. The second time it might take eight minutes. When you do it a lot of times you can do it within seconds until in time you don't have the negative thought in the first place.

You need a routine and mechanism to ensure that you are ready to cope with the stresses and strains of competitive sport until your routine becomes second nature.

Playing on a bad rink

No rink, or certainly not one that I have ever played on indoors or out, is 'unbowlable'. Spending eighty per cent of your time complaining about a green is going to do nothing to enhance your performance – or improve the surface of the green for that matter. Save your efforts and use them to concentrate fully on making the best of a 'bad' rink.

Get your weight! Indoors, there is no excuse *not* to be able to get your weight, and it is very rare outdoors that the patchiness of the green could make finding your weight so difficult that it is a lost hope. If you get your weight, which is generally far easier than finding the right line, you are on your way.

Once you have your weight it is possible that you will already be doing a better job than your opponent. However, if he/she is finding a better line, don't assume it has anything to do with the model of bowl your opponent is playing with – that is the weak way out.

Sometimes, lines are a lot easier to find on different lengths, and it may just be that you are playing a peculiar length. Furthermore (and I think this happens much more commonly than is acknowledged), players get it in their heads that the rink is tricky, when in reality it really isn't that bad.

Focus on a line, focus on a length – ignore everything else!

Gamesmanship and psychology

Your opponents may try to put you off by suggesting particular things at a certain time, and I believe that what you say can really have an impact on how your opponents perform in a game.

Obvious bad sportsmanship such as bad language or tactics to put a player off during delivery are inexcusable, but the way you communicate with your team-mates can actually have an impact on your opponents.

If I think a player who is against me struggles when shots down, I will always tell my team-mate(s) how many shots we are up. The main reason for this is not to keep my team-mates in the loop; it is more about putting the opposing player off by increasing the pressure. In no way do I believe that this is bad sportsmanship. I'm just stating a fact and the best way for my opponent to shut me up is by bowling a good bowl and cutting the score down or getting shot.

Giving away information

There is far too much discussion between a team that is shared with opponents. I would be very careful with this and use it to your advantage. It is commonplace for team-mates to shout down the rink what shot you should play or discuss the shot and 'give away' your plans at the head. You must be more subtle than this. You may have noticed the four back bowls and think it is worth a go with your final delivery, but there is no need to share information such as 'we have the best four backs' with your opponents.

Let's flip this on its head. If you have the best four back bowls but have no intention of playing the trail, then surely it would be good to make it clear to your opponents that you are 'contemplating' playing the shot. This way, they are likely to cover a shot that you weren't going to play anyway; they've wasted a bowl.

I see nothing wrong with this. I have in the past, in a highly competitive match, intimated to my number three, who is on the same wavelength as me, that I intend to draw shot. The opposing skip has then gone down to play his bowl and drawn to the head, leaving me with the chance to take the jack back to our four back bowls. Actually, I missed, but it could have got us qualified for the national finals. The opponents should have been more perceptive.

What you say and do can impact on an outcome of the game and it is important that you don't show your cards too early.

Positive talk

The way you communicate with your team is of utmost importance. I would strongly suggest that you refrain from stereotypical, critical terminologies such as 'you're tight' and talk in a more constructive manner, conducive to playing well as a team.

You may decide between yourselves that you will not tell the player at the mat how far short/wide/narrow or heavy they are. I have never really understood this practice of informing a player of the distance from the jack as it's pretty obvious from the mat. However, I am guilty of telling my team-mates where they have finished as it is the accepted practice but, in all honesty, I do wonder what it achieves. In essence, you may as well say: 'You missed it last time and have shown our opponents that you can bowl yards away from your intended target.' However, I appreciate that some, if not most, players do want their skip to tell them how far they were from their intended target. If this is your preference then keep it like that but, if you ask purely because it is the normal practice, then I would suggest you consider stopping this 'tradition'.

Positive talk between team-mates can instil a good relationship in a rink and make the player feel at ease and under less pressure.

If there's one thing I want you to take from the psychology section of this book, it is that when the bowler is ready to bowl, all he/she is thinking about is playing the next shot successfully. If anything else is in the player's head then full attention is not being paid to this absolutely essential and focal aspect, and the percentage of success is thus lowered. Talking positively can aid this.

Banning negative talk

'It is a culture in the sport but it is not prevalent in the crown green code.' This is how Tony Allcock describes the flat greens code's fascination with complaining, whereas crown green bowlers will 'get on with it'.

Extending this principle of banning 'negative talk', the English Commonwealth Games team of 2002 were under instruction by Performance Co-ordinator Tony Allcock that any negative talk would not be allowed. Thus, there was no complaining about the rink, the opponents getting all the luck, or conversely the team getting none of it.

What was the result of this? Well, out of six disciplines played, England won medals in four. Both the men's and the women's fours secured gold medals, the men's pairs achieved silver and the women's pairs acquired bronze. I think these statistics speak for themselves.

Was it purely because they didn't use negative talk that they were successful in four disciplines? Probably not. That said, it undoubtedly aided team spirit and ensured that players would not use an excuse and instead would actively go out and make things happen.

Professor Ian Maynard, along with Tony Allcock, was an integral driving force behind the principle of banning negative talk:

> For the Games we identified the 'team rules'. This included the ground rules of what we were going to do and what we weren't going to do.
>
> We knew months down the line that the greens were not going to be very good in Manchester because they had only laid them shortly before and so we had this philosophy of no whingeing – and the state of the greens was at the top of the list.

I think these rules put us ahead of the game. They were a strong team anyway and Tony balanced the expectations he had and a friendly atmosphere very well.

Tony Allcock believes it was integral to the spirit of the squad that negative talk was banned, again using crown green bowlers as an example of 'getting on with it':

Not using negative talk had the greatest impact at the Games. Again, this comes back to the 'control the controllable' principle. It is as it is and you need to get on with it! I did relate the players to the crown game on many occasions. For instance, if a streaker ran across the green, a flat green bowler would slam their bowl down, whereas a crown green bowler would send the bowl up.

Crown bowlers play outside throughout the year. They like it frosty because the green runs quick – they get on with it! If you get beat it is because somebody coped better with the conditions than you did – next time get better.

There is no point in complaining about something that cannot be rectified, and so it is imperative that you push these thoughts away and concentrate on factors that you *can* control – such as trying to get the line and weight.

Banning negative talk, in this respect, is a fundamental component of success.

Playing 'in the moment'

There's no point dwelling on or even glorifying past shots played by yourself, your team-mates or your opponents. As with all sports, you are 'playing in the moment' – your next bowl is the most important one and your concentration must not be arrested.

As Ian Maynard explains, it is essential to do this:

People know whether they have delivered a good bowl or a bad one, but you should have a process within the team to deal with that bad bowl or end so you can refocus and get on with delivering the next one. It is about getting a coping strategy that enables you to forget your last bowl and get on with the next one. This is what we call 'Parking It'.

Exactly – you are parking it! You are leaving it behind and can come back to reflect on it at a post-match analysis with your team if required. You must get back into the moment as soon as possible and make sure nothing arrests concentration!

14 The Psychology and Practicalities of Leading

There are two practical ways to play against the other lead: you can count ends won over your opposing lead, or you can just focus on playing bowls into the head time after time.

The latter, certainly for outdoor bowls, is something I would advocate. Outdoor bowls is more about 'positioning' and I believe this can start from the lead position. Indoors, I think you should change your game slightly and instead of 'ensuring' at least one bowl reaches the head, you should just try to get them as close to the jack as possible. With indoors being such a 'touch' game, if you focus too much on 'position' from an early stage, you can get in trouble more easily as your opponent(s) may find the line and length time after time. There are fewer variables in the indoor game (different grasses, paces, lines etc.) and it is generally easier to know indoors whether you have bowled a good bowl or not.

If you do everything right when you deliver a bowl indoors, you can almost guarantee you will finish near the jack, whereas outdoors this is not necessarily the same; thus positional bowls can help your team-mates later in the end if they need to reach with the very popular 'yard on' shot outdoors in the UK.

Outdoors I used to (and still do when I have the opportunity to lead) play to get bowls in the head, whether my opponent's bowls were nearer than mine being of secondary significance. I would attempt to get one on the jack and the other bowl within two feet past and positioned centrally. Thus, the number of short bowls I played could be kept to a minimum. I have played lead before in matches and played the entire game without putting a short bowl in. That said, I would suggest erring on the side of caution if you always reach as, if you are continually yards heavy, you are not contributing a great deal.

The only time I have departed from this style of play has been the three England senior trials I have played, where I have tried to get every bowl within an inch to score as many points as possible. Short bowls are a necessary collateral when trying this.

Because my main objective was to draw a front or back toucher with every bowl, I decided to play a mini-game against my opposing lead, where I would make a tally of ends won by each player so I could assess who was playing more accurately.

Generally, however, if I was playing badly at lead, I would intentionally bowl just through the head with my opening bowl and adjust accordingly, until I felt that I had acquired the pace. This is less to do with psychology and more to do with practicality, as a bowl behind is usually far more useful.

John Rednall is one of the 'great' leads.

John Rednall is one of the greatest leads in the history of the game. He is the longest-serving international in the outdoor England side and is universally respected as one of the 'greats'.

In the following article written for this book, John has outlined what he believes makes for a successful lead. Again, this isn't purely about becoming the best of the best - it is about improving your game, increasing your playing satisfaction and giving more to your team-mates:

Getting into leading

How many times have you heard comments like: 'The lead won the game for them; she was always about', or: 'Good leads are worth their weight in gold'?

The truth is, if your lead gets his or her bowls in the head, consistently, the team-mates who follow have got a much better chance of capitalizing on the foundations set by the first player and producing multiple shots through subtle trails of the jack, or by extracting the one opponent's bowl to make a count. Or, alternatively, the opponents are under pressure from the very first bowl of the end. The lead who reliably puts a bowl on the front of the jack is a highly valued resource in any standard of play.

Leading is an art form. Leads are born, not made. So what makes a good lead?

Specialist leads are dependable yet resilient; they are patient and undaunted in their role. They realize they are responsible for setting the wheels in motion of what could be a vital end or section of play. Such exponents are used to seeing the bowls that were once close to the jack being ejected – fired off, removed, turned to dust. Yet the job satisfaction spurs them on. If the opponent had to use weighted shots to remove them, then so be it. They had to waste bowls in doing so.

The mission is to put them back the next end and grind the opposition down until a breakthrough is deservedly achieved. Few games are won purely by converting heads with weight. 'Games are won from lead' is the common saying.

If the role of the lead is to create a head of bowls which has the potential to produce a multiple count of shots, then the priorities are very different from those when playing singles. I have always said that leading is not a competition to see who holds the shot after the leads have bowled. It simply does not matter. Would you rather hold shot with a single bowl in the head and the others nowhere, or be one shot down with a promising head of bowls that can be developed by the players that follow? Point made.

When we lead in pairs or triples matches, the lead's role changes slightly. There is still the need to be consistent in line or length but there will be certain trails of the jack and weighted shots ordered. In this context, the lead needs to be a good all-rounder, versatile and proficient in positioning bowls and playing aggressively if required.

So, applying this to the psychological aspects required to perform as a consistent lead, it is evident that you need to have a patient disposition, unruffled and ready to spend the whole game seeing your bowls fly out of the head.

As John states, if they are firing your bowls off, they are wasting their bowls doing so, and it puts your team on the front foot from the off.

John's style of leading correlates with mine where it is not purely about getting the shot but about building a foundation for your rink. As England's longest-serving player outdoors, his style is obviously one befitting longevity.

Insularity of leading

I believe, as a lead in triples or fours, that it is important to distance yourself from the noise and hubbub of rink play and simply focus on bowling the jack to the required position and getting your bowls close. If you do this, you have done your job and you will have greatly aided the team in its mission to win the game. You don't have to make a song and dance about it.

Being part of a noisy rink is fine, and encouraging your fellow players should be encouraged, but if your skip bowls a great bowl on the last bowl of the end and, as a lead, you get excited, I would certainly suggest calming down before casting the jack at the commencement of the next end. Getting overexcited can be detrimental to your concentration and performance.

How do you calm down if you get overexcited? Simple breathing exercises can certainly help. Take a couple of deep breaths (don't make it look obvious), focus your mind and think solely about the process of delivering the jack and where you wish it to finish.

It is imperative that your mind is cleared and your objectives are crystal clear. Still thinking about the previous end's success will mean you can be sloppy the next end; alternatively, dwelling on the fact that your fellow players did not have a good end will not help either.

Being a winner

As John Ottaway, another one of England's greatest-ever leads, stated at an England training day: 'The lead will never win you a game, but will have a large influence on the final outcome.' John is completely right. A lead will not definitively win you a match but if the player plays well, the bowls in the head will carry their weight in gold as they will consistently ensure that the opposition is trying to chase the end.

There will absolutely, definitely, be occasions when your good bowls are rendered useless by an excellent bowl by an opponent; maybe he/she trailed the jack two yards and away from your bowls, and you must be psychologically prepared for the reality that your bowls may well not stay where you put them. This will make it all the more pleasing when your bowls do stay where you put them and they were an integral part of the make-up of the end.

John Ottaway, like John Rednall, is another one of England's 'great' leads.

15 The Psychology and Practicalities of Playing Number Two

If you play number two in rinks, that means you are the least talented and least important player in the rink, right?

Not according to ex-England international Martyn Sekjer. At a recent get-together of junior international number two and three players (I was playing number two), he described us as the 'backbone' of the rink. I like this analogy. If your backbone fails or is weak, everything around it collapses and, in bowls terms, inevitably has a detrimental effect on the lead and skip. So, in what way does the number two need to be the 'backbone'?

The number two player needs to be able to 'facilitate' the lead, whether that means playing positional bowls to keep the head tight or helping him/her when they have a poor end by adopting the lead role of bowling close to the jack.

However, that is less to do with the psychology of playing two and more to do with the practicalities of the position. That said, you must also be psychologically facilitating as the number two in a rink.

You should most certainly be an essential part of the exuberance of the rink and be encouraging the rest of your team-mates, as well as constantly thinking about the board, and, if you are indoors, the card. All of this is before you even play a single bowl. For this reason, I find it perplexing that the number two position is vilified by many bowlers.

These reasons, to me, portray the reality that the number two position is the most important in a rink and, in many respects, this role should belong to the most experienced player.

I am in good company in believing the number two is arguably the most important player in the rink; this perception is backed up by England legend David Bryant, who believes the number two player is the driving force in a rink, and needs to have a varied game:

> I think the number two holds the rink together. It's nice to have a lead who puts them on the jack, but they're only human and will have their good days and their bad days. If you have got a lead who has struggled, then a lot of weight falls on the number two.
>
> The number two, in my mind, is the most important person on the rink. If you miss, when the third comes round, you're in a mess. He/she is usually the last player who has a clear route to the jack.
>
> If you have got a strong lead and strong number two against you, your back end is in for a very hard day.
>
> It's helpful if you've got a number two who is versatile and can play a range of shots, and if we are talking about an international level, it's also very helpful to have a number two who is very good at a running wood and drive.
>
> If you have to use your third with a fast wood and he/she doesn't connect, you could find yourselves in a lot of trouble. It's sometimes better for the number two to drive with their second, because if the number three misses with their first, there are only three bowls to go.

Again, looking at the terminology, David says the number two 'holds the rink together', very similar in vernacular to Martyn Sekjer's allusion to the backbone.

Just handing a bowl to a team-mate can have a positive impact.

Simple gestures

When I have played two, which has only ever been when I have played for the England juniors, I adopted an interpersonal relationship with the players, ensuring that, first and foremost, they were comfortable playing with me.

When playing two, I tended to adopt a caring, helpful approach to get the most out of the rink. Of course I am caring and helpful when I play in any position, but these aspects are heightened when playing number two. This includes other simple points that, superficially, do not appear to have a psychological aspect, but in reality they most certainly do.

At two, I would have more cloths than I needed and chalk for the three and skip if they needed it, and would go out of my way to either hand the lead his/her second bowl or push it towards him/her.

The simple gesture of handing a bowl to your lead when playing two automatically conveys the perception that the number two is friendly and helpful. I would caution against doing this for every bowl as the lead may not like this, but doing it once every two or three ends will remind the lead that the number two with him/her is courteous, helpful and paying attention. This puts the lead at ease, especially if the two players have not played with each other before, and will aid in the lead's overall performance. It's a team game – it's not just about getting the most out of your own game.

Furthermore, having enough cloths or chalk is, first and foremost, very helpful, and secondly it starts things off on a good note. It settles the players, makes them know you are thinking of them and thus improves the rink's performance. Actions that appear to just be solely helpful are actually very important to the psychological state of each player in a rink, and the number two can make a really positive input in this respect. Of course, this also comes under the Teamwork section of the book as the two are inextricably combined.

Communication

As I stress throughout this book, the number three is not the sole communicator to the skip. The three, in fours play, ultimately has to be the main spokesperson for the skip if information is required, but that does not mean that the number two cannot impart advice to the three or skip.

However, there is a very fine line between being helpful and being an irritation. Knowing your three and skip can certainly help in determining whether your input is required and appreciated or not.

If the skip is up the other end and ready to bowl, the number two should not shout up the rink as it could be seen as undermining the three, and the same applies when the three is up the other end and the skip is giving the directions. However, I feel the number two can, and indeed should, occasionally shout up the rink to reaffirm his/her team-mate's suggestion to the player on the mat.

For instance, take the following scenario:

(Number three *to skip*) 'Play the bowl out of the head for five.'

(Skip) [Pause] 'I can draw shot though.'

(Number three) 'Yes, but the bowl is worth a lot and we are five down in the game.'

(Skip) 'Hmm.'

(Number three) 'Can you see the bowl?'

(Skip) 'I can.'

(Number two, *encouragingly*) 'Come on then, you'll get this bowl out the head!'

In this instance, the two is reaffirming that the number three's suggestion is the most logical choice of shot, and the fact they are five down in the game should be more than enough of a reason to sway the skip to play the three's suggestion. Furthermore, with the rink in harmony, the skip should also have more confidence of actually getting the bowl out of the head. Here, the number two has not been disruptive or unhelpful, but rather constructive and built confidence. In using positive talk in this way, you should make the skip believe that the number three's suggestion is the best one, so the skip does not play the shot with half a mind on the that fact he/she isn't happy playing it. The affirmation by the number two that the shot is made for the skip should help give him/her a psychological boost that may be the difference between failure and success.

However, this type of interruption may not be the right approach if the skip is stubborn, or, putting it bluntly, a troublemaker. A softer approach may be needed here, with more discussion to get the required result:

(Number three *to skip*) 'Play the bowl out of the head for five.'

(Skip) [Pause] 'I can draw shot though.'

(Number three) 'Yes, but the bowl is worth a lot and we are five down in the game.'

(Skip) 'Hmm.'

(Number three) 'Can you see the bowl?'

(Skip) 'I can.'

(Number two, *to the three*) 'It might be worth asking him/her to come and have a look at the head.'

Although you're not forcing the three to take up this advice, your suggestion as the number two seems to be a perfectly sensible one. If the three shouts up for the skip to look at the head, the skip has two choices in reality. He/she can either say: 'No, I can see it', and play the shot the rink want the skip to play, or: 'OK, I'll have a look.' If the skip simply says: 'I'm not playing it!', then I would suggest that you look for a new skip.

By coming to have a look at the head, the number three, with the help of his/her team-mates, can gently persuade the skip that the trail is the right shot. This scenario is also ideal as differences in ideas can be ironed out quietly, rather than shouting up the rink to each other.

Disagreeing with the three

However, there will be other instances in a discussion where the number two may need to raise and address certain points with the number three, maybe in order to 'back up' the skip.

If you slightly change the scenario and make it a six-rink match, it can mean that the skip's shot is probably the most sensible one:

(Number three *to skip*) 'Play the bowl out of the head for five.'

(Skip) [Pause] 'I can draw shot though.'

(Number two, *aside, to three*) 'We're three up over all the rinks and if he/she takes the jack back, we'll drop a three.'

(Three, *to the two*) 'True, but we are five down in our game.'

(Two, *to three*) 'Yes, but it may not be worth the risk as the overall game is what matters most.'

Note that the conversation has not been allowed to drag in this instance. Obviously, intonation is important and you don't want to sound aggressive or demeaning; it is important you address the situation with due care.

Ultimately, you want to be an effective playing partner with your entire rink, and it is important that you have the full respect of the three and skip in fours play, as if you fail with your bowls (which you are bound to do in the course of a game), you will need them to step in. Having 'favourites' in the rink will do you no favours, and no matter how well you may play personally, a rink in disharmony is asking for a fall.

Focusing at two

All of these finer details distract from the obvious: the need for the number two to play well to help his/her rink out. There is no psychology needed here – excessively short bowls are completely useless and I don't need to go into detail as to why that is the case. Consolidating a lead's bowl that is close to the jack by putting a front bowl in is leaving you exposed to a dead draw or a running shot – you could have improved the head instead of bowling short.

So, how do you play well when you have all of these other factors to include when playing at two?

When I am passing the lead his/her second bowl and saying 'well bowled' or 'next time' or 'that's good there', etc., I am also focusing on getting myself prepared to bowl. By taking an interest in the lead's bowls, you know the head and usually don't have to ask the skip anything. You can judge what kind of role you will be playing from an early stage and, if the lead's opener is wayward, you can be prepared to play the lead role. If the lead's second bowl is close, you will still be playing a similar shot anyway as you will need more than one bowl in the head. So, you are preparing yourself for the shot you will play whilst also being helpful to your lead; you are the ultimate multi-tasker.

Preparation

Whilst we are on preparation, it is important to note that you must also be prepared to play whatever shot your skip tells you to. You can, of course, discuss the shot if you are unsure but, ultimately, you must play the shot the *skip* has told you to play and show no signs of discontent before you play it, because if you do so then this will only create a bad atmosphere. Even if the shot is not something you think you should be playing, there may be a very good reason why he/she wants you to play it. I hear many of you now saying: 'Yes, because the skip wants to keep the good hand for his/herself.' Usually, this isn't the case, but if your skip is keeping the best hand free for him/herself, I would suggest you politely address this.

Thus, the stereotype that the 'new' bowler should play at number two is clearly one I do not advocate. I would suggest a new bowler plays lead; if he/she has a problem casting the jack then practice is required. Once a new player gets used to drawing close time after time, he/she can explore playing in other positions if desirous of a change, and the number two option may be a possibility, but such a player should have practised a whole range of other shots during roll-ups.

Triples play

In triples, you really are the backbone of the rink as the two and you must play as such. Usually, the number two will stand up with the skip and, to an extent, you can leave the lead to his/her business, exchanging little more than pleasantries and words of encouragement as you pass each other. However, you must have a good relationship with the skip, and I would advocate, when the shot is not obvious, bouncing ideas off each other. The lead may also be more vocal in triples as he/she will spend a portion of the game solely with the skip when you are down the other end on the mat and then with you when the skip is at the other end, so you and the skip must respect the opinions of the lead.

Friend to the rink

Ultimately, when you play number two, you want to be 'friends' with everyone. This means listening, conducting yourself in a proper manner, being helpful in whatever you do and successfully supporting the lead when he/she has had a good end, or backing the lead up when he/she has had a bad end by adopting the lead role and getting your bowls near the jack. If you can blend all these aspects together successfully, you will be an extremely effective number two.

16 The Psychology and Practicalities of Playing Number Three

Playing number three in a rink, or, as Tony Allcock succinctly puts it, playing the 'vice-skip' role, completes the backbone of the rink.

You must be in the right psychological frame of mind to play the position well. I have found this the most difficult position to occupy, as being a 'facilitating' player at two seems to come naturally to me, but, at three, I have found in the past that I have not been one hundred per cent sure what I am supposed to be doing.

Tony Allcock explains that it is a difficult position as you have to be malleable, depending on who you are playing with:

> The third position can be many roles and these roles can change, depending on the unit in which you are placed. I would call it a chameleon position. You have to transform and mould yourself into that role, unless the unit has been moulded around you. The other roles tend to be more straightforward. The third position is dependent predominantly on the relationship with the skip.
>
> Some thirds can't cope with the autocratic approach and yet some absolutely need it. Some skips prefer the third to have that approach.

Relationship with the skip

In essence, you are what the skip tells you to be. Whilst it is important that you appreciate and encourage the front-end players in your rink, the most important link in the rink for you is the one with the skip.

If you've been playing for thirty years and you find yourself playing with a skip who is new to the position, don't be overbearing and *do not* dominate the head. Even the most placid skip, if he/she is new to the position, will wish to exert overall authority on a rink. Players can forget that. Although being helpful and vocal is conducive to an effective overall team performance, the skip is ultimately in charge.

On the flip side, the skip must acknowledge that, to get the most out of his/her players, a warm and friendly atmosphere where discussion is encouraged should prevail.

Playing the shots

I believe this is where the number three position can become blurry and it can be very frustrating for the player.

I suggest you take advice from the skip in this and all other instances, but you should not be afraid to tell the skip what your preference of shot is. After all, it is the player playing the shot who knows which option he/she prefers.

Most importantly, with the number two and skip positions as well, when you have chosen what shot to play (there may be three, four or even five options available) there must be no confusion about which shot you are playing and your focus must be fully on the task in hand – playing and executing your shot to perfection. Having multiple options in your head will be psychologically detrimental as you will not be able to focus fully.

Positives of playing number three

In many respects, you have to ensure that you are 'in the zone'. By the very nature of the game, you will probably not communicate much with the lead and two until after you have completed your bowls, as you are at the other end and the skip will be giving instructions to both of them, so you can make the most of this time available by getting in the right state of mind during the end.

It is like a game of chess. You, like the skip, have to be mindful that the head could change at any moment and be ready to play any shot and play it perfectly, no matter how difficult it may be. By staying perceptive and engaged in the end and preparing for every eventuality, you will have given yourself the best chance to play the shot required.

Playing the shot

If the skip, as is the nature of the game generally nowadays, tells you to play the shot 'you feel most confident playing', accept this invitation. However, bear in mind, for instance, that if you play a full drive and miss the head completely, you have not helped the skip at all. At the same time, if you elect the dead draw and you are down, is there a danger that if you finish short you will only add to the mess for your skip? You must be selfless when you think of this and consider the percentages. The best option may be a shot which, even if it doesn't turn out exactly as you hoped, will still help you with your second bowl.

The vice-skip

The number three is not just the 'facilitator' for the skip, and this is what Tony Allcock alludes to when he describes the number three as the 'vice-skip', a term commonly employed in Canada for a number three player.

When the skip goes off the rink, the number three must stand in as skip and direct accordingly and naturally – the number three should not look uncomfortable or indecisive when filling this role, but should be ready to give useful advice if needed.

Furthermore, the number three should not be afraid to tell the skip what shot should be played if the skip looks indecisive, and should not be afraid to suggest to the skip that an alternative shot could be the better one. If this leads to confrontation, the likeliest reason for this is that the skip still lives in the Dark Ages of the sport of bowls.

At three, you aren't the main man/woman. That said, your relationship with the skip is integral to the performance of the rink.

You need to get in the right psychological mindset to follow instructions and give instructions. It's not easy to do this effectively.

17 The Psychology and Practicalities of Playing Skip

Leader. Boss. Authoritarian. Idol? You need to strike a good balance as a skip – your opponents should fear you, they should notice your supreme confidence and effective man or woman management of your rink to get the most out of your team, but you *must* make sure that this confidence does not come at a price in your rink. Yes, you are the leader, but the best leaders listen.

Getting yourself prepared as a skip

Complacency breeds failure. If you are an established skip and believe you know everything about the position and how to get the most out of your players, you will fail.

You have to continue learning from others and I would also advocate occasionally playing down the pecking order for the purpose of looking at the general practice of other skips and seeing whether they have an approach you would/wouldn't like to adopt.

Using the number three

If I am skipping and have an experienced number three, I actively encourage that player to occasionally take control of the head and give directions. This is very different from passing 'power' over to the three – I am delegating as I believe that this will give the number three an amount of empowerment and keep him/her engaged with the front-end play.

If the shot is obvious, I will just tell the player at the other end what to play. If it is not obvious I will always ask the number three and, if I agree, then that is the shot we tell the lead, or more regularly, the two, to play. If we disagree we can give the player at the other end two options. If we agree on one option, if he/she wants to, the number three can shout the direction down the rink. This keeps the three engaged and, although it somewhat contradicts what I said in my previous chapter on the point that as number three you don't have to communicate that much with the front end, I believe it is good to keep the three on his/her toes.

Conversely, if the number three is inexperienced, you can take two approaches. The first is to take the burden of instruction off the player entirely so that he/she can concentrate on playing well and purely focus on his/her bowls. However, I would not advocate this. I would occasionally ask for advice as, in my opinion, psychologically, this will make the player feel involved in the rink and that his/her opinion really matters. Two brains are always better than one anyway. This is all adding to a successful team dynamic where every player feels respected. I think the problem with not discussing with the three, whether they are experienced in that position or not, is that they can feel isolated and not involved in the team. One major problem with this is that the essential communicative skills conducive to good harmony in a rink can be somewhat jaded as the number three can spend much of the end 'out of the loop'. Keeping him/her engaged is of paramount importance.

If you are a skip who prefers an 'I'm in charge' approach, it really is important that your team-mates are all fine with this, as it is old-fashioned nowadays.

Preparing for your shot

As mentioned earlier, bowls is like a game of chess, and you hold the power to be King or Queen. It is important that you watch the end. This is essential inasmuch as your team-mates will appreciate that you look interested, and this will boost them psychologically, but also, by keeping an eye on the end, you can get an insight into the tactics your opponents are employing and also, more simply, what line you have to give it.

After directing your players, you must be ready to phase out everything and focus on your shot. Don't put too much pressure on yourself – it will probably result in you missing your shot.

18 Psychological Preparation in a Singles Match

Marmite – that's the best way to describe singles. You either love it or hate it. The liberation of being able to select your own shots and play uninhibitedly can be a major positive for some people, but a lack of guidance and, in some cases, belief, can put people off entering singles disciplines in the first place.

Your psychological approach in singles play is different from team games. It is important that you prepare according to how you would usually like to prepare, but at the same time addressing the reality that the game is as much about a game of wits between you and your opponent as it is about ability.

During the game

Your opponent may try to get the psychological edge by playing to your weaknesses. For instance, if you are a fast player, your opponent may decide (if he/she has any sense) to slow the game down, visit the head regularly and generally do anything within the laws of the sport to counteract your desire for speed. This is not bad etiquette; it is about 'playing the game', and if your opponent has started the mind games, I would condone playing him/her at their own game, but make sure it is not to the detriment of your own game.

Talking

It's good to talk. That said, if your opponent knows you like fewer interruptions, he/she might play to that and natter to you. This is a very difficult position to be in. You want to be polite, courteous and friendly, but this could be disadvantageous to your performance.

You have to balance the need for you to play at your best with playing in the spirit of the game and understanding that the sport of bowls is a social game, as well as a competitive one.

The player facing you may not even be putting you off intentionally; he/she may purely be being chatty and friendly. However, if it is really putting you off, you may have to give simple answers to any questions posed.

Don't be afraid to be a little cold; you can talk as much as you like when you have a drink after the game, but don't 'burn your bridges' and get a reputation for being sullen or too serious. It's a balance you will have to address yourself.

Preparation

As stated in previous chapters on how to prepare appropriately, I would suggest that you prepare for a singles match in the same way as you would for a team game – however you feel most comfortable.

That said, because of the isolated nature of singles, it may be good to prepare by spending time on your own, rather than communicating with others before the match. This may well mean that you just stay in your car for five minutes to get away from the hubbub of the club.

Mindset

You have to believe you will beat your opponent. If you can't believe this, then you are inevitably going to lose. You must be very careful with your psychological state of mind. You must be wary of your opponent, but not overawed. It's a balance that must be struck in order for you to be in the right state of mind to face your opponent.

19 Psychological Advantage Over Your Opponent

'Play the game.' If someone gets worked up if they miss a shot, really stress how very unlucky they were and that you can't believe that they found 'that gap' or 'kept on running', etc. This will hopefully have the desired effect of working your opponent further into a frenzy.

If your opponent is complaining about the surface, whether indoors or out, you are at an automatic advantage. You've got him/her where you want. This is even better in team games because someone's disgruntlement about the quality of a surface can rub off on his/her team-mates, and it is very possible they will all mutter about the surface rather than sticking to the task in hand - getting on with the game.

If they are complaining that you are finding a better line than them, keep them thinking that. It may well be true but, in the majority of instances, it is because your opponent is not playing very well and is looking for an excuse.

Your opponent may genuinely believe it is the lines, in which case you should keep them believing this untruth. Simple remarks such as: 'Wow, I can't believe that bent so much' or: 'That's ridiculous – that should have got down to the jack' will confirm to them that they are being unlucky and that it is the surface that is conspiring against them. Your empathy and sympathy will be welcomed by them, but, in reality, you are just adding to their demise and psychological disadvantage. In being empathetic, you are doing them no favours at all. Who cares if they are all full of excuses after the match? You are in the next round, they are not.

As an aside, if they are complaining about your bowls being too narrow, ignore them. You have purchased and are using a perfectly legal set of bowls (hopefully) and it is up to them to employ the correct tactics to thwart the threat that your tight-running bowls hold.

How to behave when playing badly

On the flip side, in order to gain an advantage over your opponent, you must keep a poker face.

If players in your team are playing badly, you don't need that reaffirming by hand gestures and overt movements from the person who played a bad bowl, or by you waving your hands around either. That said, in team games, I would advocate a simple apology to your team-mates if you play a bad bowl, otherwise they may think you are not interested in the game. Psychology works both ways.

Do not fall for your opponents' empathy. If they say they were surprised the bowl did not drop, etc., it's most likely a ruse. You can agree with them verbally, but don't believe it - just make sure your next bowl is better.

Bowlers continually want to feel sorry for themselves, even at the highest level, and I find it crazy that in the twenty-first century, with so much information available on the psychology of sport, bowls has not moved forward in this regard.

20 Using Psychology to Overcome Your Nemesis

Everyone has got a nemesis: 'I just can't beat him!' Well, let me tell you, if you have enough talent, then there really is no such thing as 'can't'. It is a negative word and should not be used in bowls, or any sport, for that matter.

Starting with such negativity will only add to the myth that your nemesis 'cannot' be beaten.

Getting the right mindset

First, you should just concentrate on playing as well as you can. If your opponent gets a piece of luck, do not be dispirited and disheartened; it won't help you.

Just focus on getting every bowl close and block out who you are playing and the fact you have a poor record against him/her.

Ian Maynard believes that you should, most of the time, focus on the 'moment'. The only way you can alter the result is by doing it in the moment!

> There are two distinct ways of playing your 'nemesis'. The first one is to not think about your opponent at all – just disregard who they are. Be totally focused on your game because ultimately it is usually playing your game well that wins the matches.
>
> The other way that works for some people is disrupting the opposition and that is by stopping your opponent playing their natural game. It is about identifying which of these two ways works best for you. For me, 98 per cent of people will just focus on playing to their strengths. Very few people will go out there to play the person. If you do this then you will tend to remember what went wrong before when you played this person last time and you will probably end up losing again.
>
> You should do what I call a 'process orientation' to a game, rather than an 'outcome orientation'. Players can think so much about winning and losing that they are forgetting to use the process involved to play at their best. This includes the delivery and strategic and tactical processes. Winning is not 'in the moment'. Winning is in the future so you have to come back to the moment.

Ultimately, when you get into focusing on your nemesis, you are already in a losing frame of mind.

On a slightly different tack, Tony Allcock believes you must dissect what went wrong the last time you played this opponent and use that as a starting point:

This is where I believe you need psychological assistance. Beating Willie Wood was a big problem for me. He was possibly psychologically above me when we started out.

I think you need to analyse how you lost last time to see how you are going to find some rationale of how you are going to approach it this time.

The two accounts of Ian and Tony differ slightly, but both can be deployed. As Ian states, play your own game, but Tony's acknowledgement that you should analyse what went wrong last time is also invaluable. Do both, get in a positive frame of mind and 'risk to win'.

Reverse psychology

It may well be that your opponent has two mindsets when playing you.

First, and most likely, the player is going to be complacent, and with complacency comes sloppiness. He/she will think that their first bowl doesn't need to be that near and that, no matter what happens, he/she will win.

It is up to you to use this to your advantage, most notably by playing well. In either a singles match or team game, by the time this 'nemesis' realizes he/she has a game on his/her hands, it may well be too late.

However, it is also plausible that your opponent is nervous, knowing that they have always beaten you. The player may feel that he/she will be expected to win, and this weight of expectation could well hang heavily on the player. Getting a good start against this opponent will sow seeds of doubt in their mind and, before you know it, you have won. (Conversely, I must stress that a poor start may well settle the player's nerves and will most likely result in you losing.)

As Andy Thomson reiterates, it is your mindset when you play your 'nemesis' that will have a strong impact on the final result:

Go out and believe that this is the time you will beat your nemesis. If you go into the match with a negative attitude, you will lose the game. It is as simple as that. It is imperative that you block out all negative vibes and focus on playing as well as you can. Maybe then, you can topple your nemesis.

21 The Psychology of a Winner

All of the psychological techniques I have suggested you should/can implement to give you that extra edge add up to a specific formula: it gives you the psychology of a winner!

As is stated in many, if not all sports, winning becomes a 'habit' and by approaching the game in the right psychological state of mind, you are increasing your chances of success.

Preparation before a match, psychological techniques used during a match and even an analysis of your performance after a match technically, tactically and psychologically, will enable you to become a better player.

Professor Maynard explains that being a 'winner' is about knowing yourself and your strengths and weaknesses as much as anything else:

A lot of it is to do with awareness. If you know what your strengths are and are playing to your strengths, you are giving yourself a better chance. You need to be doing the right things all the time.

There's no guidebook but more importantly there's no guesswork either. You have turned over all of the stones. You should always be looking for the edge, whether this is psychologically, physically or tactically.

Tony Allcock strongly believes it is an innate hatred of defeat that gives you a 'winner' psychology:

In all honesty, I believe people who are actually not too bothered if they win or lose will struggle to be high achievers.

Our sport, for many years, crucified competitors and those who actually hated losing.

If you are putting the work in, you give yourself a chance. There needs to be a goal.

A true winner's mentality is something that can be acquired and manufactured, but it is also usually there within you. A real winner is always the person who gets really upset when they lose.

Tony is not advocating being a bad loser here, but is rightly emphasizing that the result really needs to 'matter', as it would with any other sport.

Tactical

22 Introduction to Tactical Approaches

Don't play the glory shot unless necessary. It doesn't usually go to plan and just makes your team-mates think you are playing for yourself.

It is true that tactical ineptitude will ensure, more often than not, that the outcome of your game is a negative one. No matter what happens, common sense should always prevail. If your opponents have five back bowls and you hold three shots, don't build up the head any more, put a back bowl in! If a bowl can go out of the head for a number of shots and there is little danger, play the bowl out! Simple, isn't it?

Well, I would suggest that there is a grey area to tactical approaches and I believe the game is evolving to an extent where the running bowl is becoming, in many instances, the first choice of shot for many players when in trouble.

Outdoors, this is most certainly the case, where playing a running bowl on many surfaces in the UK would require you to play with a none-too-dissimilar line to a draw, making the running bowl an obvious option when in trouble. Indoors, however, is not so simple and requires a greater deal of thought and accuracy. On many indoor surfaces, it may be that the draw/drive option would be the best.

South Africans and Australians do not mess about. If you get close to the jack (even if you are leading in some circumstances), you'll soon see it hit off. One of the reasons for this, particularly in Australia, is because the greens are so fast and the 'yard on' shot or runner is virtually impossible; it is most likely to be the most difficult shot to execute.

You can already see that there is a distinct grey area. Furthermore, the subject of 'tactics' is so subjective that unless you are getting it horribly wrong, there is no real 'right' or 'wrong' answer.

Take the example illustrated by the following image. It looks like a very simple trail shot for the player with the red bowls to make three, with a nice couple of feet of pace. However, if the rink has proved to be very tricky, with a yard of pace, either swinging away viciously or holding a line, you may choose to play a more attacking trail, or a drive.

Furthermore, is the line to the jack somewhat hidden on the backhand? If you drive, you could take both red bowls out, but this would be very unlucky. You would be more likely to knock the green bowls out or take the jack right through to your back bowl.

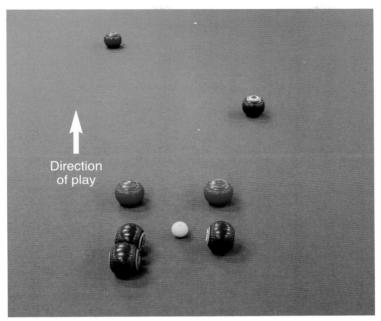

Direction
of play

A backhand or forehand drive for the player with red bowls might not be the
'prettiest' shot here, but it might well be the most sensible one, depending on the
circumstances.

That said, if the green bowl player has another bowl to play, could a drive
open up a possibility of a worse result for the red bowl player than if the said
person played the draw? It very much depends on the circumstances and you
only ever play the 'wrong' shot if it doesn't go to plan.

23 Playing to Your Strengths

You cannot fire with every bowl in a game, or draw every single time you are
in trouble and be successful. On occasions, you *will* have to play a range of
shots and thus it may be that you cannot *always* play to your strengths.

However, within reason, only you can truly know what shot to play. If you
have played six backhand drives and hit them all but missed on the forehand,
play your next drive on the backhand, even if it looks like a forehand shot.

I recommend that, when playing with a new rink, each team-mate acquires as much information as possible about the others. The skip or three is then less likely to ask a team-mate to play a shot he/she is uncomfortable with.

It may be that you usually have a preference of shot – you prefer playing the backhand to the forehand, you don't like playing running bowls, etc. and it is essential that, before you play your shot, you have addressed these issues and are at ease when you come to deliver your bowl.

Take the following example: you are the red bowl player, three down and struggle playing the yard-on shot but like to drive, but you also back yourself to draw the shot.

Here, as the player with the red bowls, all three options are sound choices, highlighting the futility of trying to 'learn' tactics.

In my mind, all three options – draw, trail shot and drive – are available here. If you draw, you secure the one, and if you are accidentally slightly heavy that is not a problem as you can use a green bowl to come off. You have eight inches to draw shot and may be confident of doing exactly that. However, you also have the option of playing a runner to trail the jack back to the other red bowl two-and-a-half feet behind, and a slice on the jack either side is okay too, but what is the point of playing the shot if you don't feel comfortable doing it? The drive seems plausible – the jack back secures a score of two if yours goes through and, at worst, you will push a green bowl through and won't be any worse off than you are currently. If you miss the intended target of the jack slightly, there is every chance you could take out one, if not two, of your opponent's bowls, or use them to go onto the jack. Here, if I were driving, the forehand looks a better option to me, but if you are better at the backhand drive, play that.

In this instance, it is about choosing what shot *you* feel is the right one for you. Thus, there is no real Holy Grail booklet about what shot to play and when. Use your common sense and nous and choose your shot accordingly.

24 Playing the Percentages

Tactically speaking, the main thing I would always suggest you do is play the percentages.

'Playing the percentages' does not always necessarily suggest you are playing a shot that could make the maximum impact, or have the greatest chance of success. It can also mean that you are building the head and increasing the chances of a team-mate getting a better result later in the end, or that you get an increased percentage chance with your next bowl.

Take the six illustrations on the following pages as examples of an end and you will see that there are a number of options available and not one of them can be proved to be '*wrong*'. A shot is never the 'wrong' option if you get the right result. That said, you can certainly help yourself by playing the percentage shot.

Let us take a scenario. It is a singles match and 17–17. I will analyse the typical thought process of Players A and B. Of course, the situation is hypothetical but it does present a perfectly plausible case study to work from.

Player A has just bowled the bowl in the first illustration. Player B might be good at driving and favour getting it, but realistically Player B will have about a thirty per cent chance of getting the intended target – it is more likely to go wrong than go right. It will also mean that playing a draw with his/her next delivery will be more difficult as Player B will have lost the pace in his/her arm.

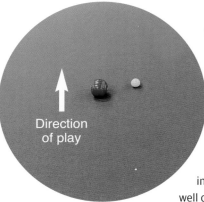

Here, as it is 17–17, Player B will not want to bowl short, but won't want to be too far away from the jack either, as that will give Player A a better chance of drawing in another.

Thus, here, Player B should play a dead draw, but bear in mind that a short bowl will be no good.

Player B could follow Player A down on the backhand and use the bowl, but, in this scenario, Player B has played really well on the forehand in this game, so would see no reason to change just yet.

With the delivery from Player B finishing slightly wide, it is not shot but it is 'in the head'. At this early stage, as Player A, you would not be thinking too much about position. Player A would want to increase the pressure on the other player, but not widen the head if possible. It would almost be a scenario where Player A would want to get close but not too close. Player A should play backhand again (the first bowl was good) with the intention of being slightly wide, trying to push the bowl onto the jack, or go round and finish slightly past the head. If Player A is slightly wide or tight, he/she should still get a good result.

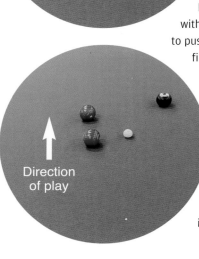

Player A would be happy with this result on the whole. Drawing round the shot bowl, this has finished well and in the count. As Player B, would you drive yet? No! Player B has a decent bowl a couple of feet behind and it will be difficult for Player A to beat it with his/her other two deliveries. Besides, if Player B drives and takes his/her own bowl out, Player B will definitely be three down when coming to play the third delivery and then panic could set in.

On the face of it, and in most circumstances, Player B would switch hands and play a reaching draw bowl with a number of 'percentages' in the player's favour on the backhand. Player B can stop on the shot bowl and push it through for shot – it is not perfect as Player A will then have two through the head, but it is still a better situation. If Player B is wide, he/she can sit off the second bowl or if it finishes inside the shot bowl, Player B can trail the jack for two and put Player A on the back foot, making his/her first two deliveries pretty useless. However, in this scenario, Player B has played really well on the forehand throughout the game, so should he/she change so soon? In this instance, I suggest going with your instinct (personally, I would switch), but Player B and I don't share the same tactical brain. In this instance, Player B tries one more go on the forehand. Even if Player B misses, it will hopefully finish as another decent bowl just behind the head.

Player A could be thinking: 'Yes, I hold two. I can continue what I am doing and draw in again on the backhand and if Player B misses the next two deliveries, I will win.' However, this does not take into account the percentages of your opponent. Player B has played a poor bowl, bowling wide of the head, and in hindsight should have switched hands, but it has still finished in a decent position. The likeliest outcome of Player A choosing to continue bowling in the head on the backhand is a chat at the bar with Player B about how he/she should have covered the jack trail. If Player B changes his/her hand, this is a real possibility.

Thus, Player A has to change his/her hand here onto the forehand. There's no point drawing another in and making a nice target for Player B to trail the jack and leave Player A in trouble.

Direction of play

Player A would certainly not want to be short and so would, in an ideal world, want to reach right up to Player B's two bowls. Counting would be a bonus, but the fact that it is a back bowl and somewhere near the green bowls is the major priority.

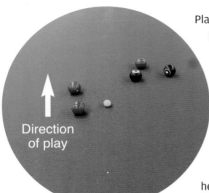

Direction of play

Player B now has the luxury of knowing he/she is not going to lose the game this end. The bowl has travelled slightly too far to count and bent just inside the wide green wood of Player B's widest bowl but has finished in a good place.

Enough messing around on the forehand – Player B missed with the first two; it's time to play a slight trail of the jack on the backhand. Player B knows he/she can't drop four now so can afford to attack a little more. Two feet of weight is enough and if Player B gets the perfect result then Player B knows he/she can make three and really put the pressure on Player A.

Driving here would, if Player B hit it, be a satisfactory result, but if Player B is confident here then he/she should play for the trail shot to the other two bowls. Player B can drive with his/her last if he/she feels it necessary. With a trail shot, Player B still has the contingency of stopping on the shot or second bowl and so his/her options are still varied.

Player B has got the perfect result. Player A had done all he/she could and so should not be angry with him/herself. The back bowl was just slightly heavier than intended and it took a fantastic bowl to make the three. Player B was just as likely to get one of the less desired results.

Direction of play

Now, Player A doesn't want to drop a four, and taking his/her back bowl out would give Player B a much easier chance to draw four, but Player A's bowl is well hidden and it will be quite hard to beat it to draw in to limit the damage. Player A doesn't want to gift his/her opponent the game, but it would be very unlucky to make the head worse by electing to drive. If Player A takes his/her back bowl out, it will be because he/she has hit one of Player B's bowls onto it, so it will be really unlikely that Player A will remain three down as Player B's bowl(s) should also leave the head. Player A cannot play for every contingency and, to some extent here, it's time to take a risk and play a drive in an attempt to achieve 'damage limitation'. Player A would not expect to get shot out of the drive but if, at the completion of the end, he/she has only dropped one or two, it will have been a successful shot and the percentages will have been played well. The best result, and a likely one if Player A hits the shot bowl, is a dead end. Player A could play the draw but, in all likelihood, it won't finish nearer than the three shots or his/her nearest bowl, making it *not* the percentage shot to play.

There is also an option for a 'yard-on' shot to stop on one of the three shots or push the jack through, but it isn't easy. Furthermore, if Player A does push the jack through to his/her own back bowl, this could conceivably leave a shot for Player B to knock Player A's out with a controlled weight shot for four to win the match.

Thus, in reality, this shot requires a drive.

Whether or not Player A hit the drive, we will never know, but the case study shows, even at an early stage, that there are many options available to a player.

Grade your chances

When you next play a game, really think about whether you are playing the 'percentage' shot; think about what percentage of success you believe you have of getting a beneficial result. Also bear in mind what the ramifications are if you miss. Will your bowl still have a chance of being useful if it misses the intended target?

Don't just always assume that the draw bowl is the best shot, and don't turn your nose up at an opponent who plays a more attacking game than you; adapt accordingly and don't be afraid to attack yourself if necessary.

You need to balance the chance of success with how useful the bowl will be if you miss. Obviously, if it is the last delivery of the end, I suggest you play the shot that is most likely to get a positive result as, if you miss, it doesn't matter where your bowl finishes.

For example – and I have seen this on many occasions outdoors – you may have two yards to draw shot with the last bowl of the end or, if you take the shot bowl out and stay, you claim three. This usually happens when the opposing skip plays an attacking shot and the jack goes back.

First, you have to play a well-timed shot for your bowl to stay in the head and count, and a one-bowl target is a lot harder to play than a draw to within two yards of the jack. Don't play for glory; play the shot that gives you the best chance.

Realistically, as a player of good standard, you will be looking at the following percentages of success:

Ditch the jack by mistake · · · · · · · · · · · 5%
Take bowl out and make a three · · · · · 10%
Take bowl out and make a two · · · · · · 20%
Draw shot · 90%

Surely it is best to play the percentage shot, keep the momentum and feel the pace of the green? Okay, if the bowl is worth seven and you have last bowl, then you have to balance the fact that you could make a match-winning contribution with one delivery with the percentage chance of success, but, for a maximum of three shots, it is not worth it.

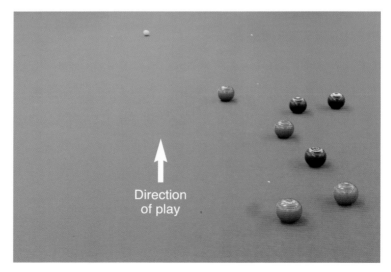

Here, the 'sensible' shot is the draw for the green bowl player, even though it is the last bowl of the end (singles match). You can push the bowl through to the ditch for two or three if you stay in the count, but the draw is a much easier shot.

Take the following example of the player using red bowls. The jack through looks lovely for the red bowl player, and that might be the primary target.

However, what happens if the player is one millimetre tight of taking the jack? He/she will get absolutely nothing. The bowl, apart from possibly being a decent back bowl if there are any more bowls left, is useless. Playing for the jack here leaves the player with very little scope. The shot to play here is definitely one where the player would want to be wide rather than tight.

The red player could get lucky and use the far wing bowls - that means missing the intended target by quite a way but still getting the desired result of cutting down or getting shot. In doing this, the player is not playing for luck - he/she is acknowledging that if he/she bowls wide of the head, that is a possible result. If he/she gets inside the bowls, the player will be in the head anyway. I know that if I had a choice between bowling a lovely bowl and missing the jack by half an inch or 'using the furniture' to get the desired result, I would sit on the sofa every time!

Outrageous pieces of fortune are not what I would hope for (certainly not verbally), and it is very important that, if you miss what you are playing for entirely and get a very fortunate result, you apologize to your opponents. If they don't reciprocate that when they are fortunate then you just have to excuse their ignorance.

Bowling tight here on the backhand would be a criminal offence!

Take a look at this scenario. Obviously, a trail of six inches is required to make three shots for the red bowl player. It's elementary, isn't it? No, it's not, because the red bowl player is blocked out of a perfect trail. Both forehand and backhand are blocked off from a lovely tickle on the jack. The player may not have the best back but I would forget about the lovely little trail for three and get the jack out of the head and start again. The red player can't go worse than two down with a horrid result if he/she hits the target area from what I can see, so the *percentage* shot is to play through it with a runner or drive. If it is the last

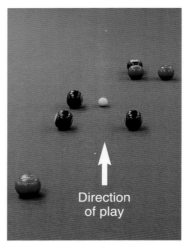

A draw or trail is out of the question here. The shot played needs to be a runner or drive to play the percentages.

bowl of the end, the player can kill it or go through with the jack and still claim one, and if there are more bowls to come, the red player will have opened the head up at worst.

The red bowl player could draw, but, assuming that the game is close, there is no point in trying to get around the green bowl on the forehand, or just inside/outside the short bowl, because the chances of success are minute.

Drawing round the green bowl on the forehand to get shot with a dead weight is *possible*, but it is very likely that the red player will miss and it really isn't worth playing it.

In this instance, if the red player is playing with more pace, he/she has a plethora of favourable results. When I say favourable, I mean that it is better than the three shots down he/she currently is.

Let's say the red player elects a backhand runner. First, a direct hit of the jack will see it go somewhere, probably back, and this will leave the player with plenty of space if he/she has another bowl, or one down at worst.

The three counting bowls, although against, can be pushed around the head and cause havoc, or the red player can use the edge off any of them to great effect as well. This is another case of 'using the furniture' - there is no luck in getting this result. If the red player gets this, he/she was in the area and deserves something for it. The forehand runner is also an option and the red player does not have to worry about hitting his/her own short bowl.

The possibilities are endless!

25 Building the Head

The age-old tactic of 'building the head' is a dying art. Seriously, I believe that society has had a part in this. In this world of multimedia instantaneousness, we expect to have everything we want as soon as possible.

Bowls is no different; building a head around an opponent's shot bowl is, for many, not the preferential shot. The first choice is to attack it.

The irony of this is that you limit the chances you have of being very successful at securing large counts. It is almost easier to claim a large count when you crowd the head, make it as difficult as possible for your opponents to get another bowl in the area, and take the bowl out at a later stage when your opponents have fewer opportunities to reclaim the head for themselves.

Take the following example: you are playing number two in a rink game, with the green bowls representing one team and red the other (see below). Yes, as a red bowler, you could play anything from a yard to a drive here and

As a red team player, build the head, stop your opponents getting in and take the bowl out at a later stage.

do so with some success, possibly flicking the shot out of the head to leave you with three, but do you really achieve anything by playing such a positive shot so early? For starters, there's still room to draw the shot. Put another in the head, crowd it out and play it out later if it becomes apparent that it is worth a large count.

The number two

I have explained hitherto that the number two position is arguably the most psychologically demanding and I also believe that the tactics deployed by the skip to the number two can make or break a rink.

If the head looks tricky, it may be that the number two is advised to drive at the head, and this may well be the most sensible shot. However, if the head is tight when the number two drives, the chances of hitting the head are slimmer. It could be that a slightly wide bowl slightly in front of the shot may make it easier to play a shot later on. However, the bowl can't be too short or in the line as this could get in the way. Again, this paradox is what makes the number two position so difficult.

Furthermore, a simple yard-on shot could also have the desired effect of spreading the head, and if you miss, your team has a decent back bowl. These are the decisions the two and skip have to make.

The number three

Even at three you should not automatically think that, because there are fewer chances to drastically alter a negative head, you should automatically attack.

Again, building a head can serve two functions. It can lessen the probability that you will drop a big count and it may present an opportunity to attack later on. However, overt negativity will also have a detrimental effect and can put too much pressure on the rink. It truly is a balancing act and I feel that, if you are unsure what shot to play and are comfortable playing a range of shots, you should choose the attacking option.

The skip

Now, there is no point in 'building a head' if you are skipping. If you are shots up and make the head wider, you have not helped matters, and if you are down and continue to build the head up but not cut down, you'll lose the end.

If it is a fours match, you evidently have two chances. If there is nothing else on and you are completely blocked out, it is wise to 'sacrifice' one bowl by implementing a full drive to open up the head to give yourself a chance with the second delivery. Take the rather overt example in the picture and pretend that there are more bowls in and around the head. If the skip were bowling for the reds here, there would be no point trying to build the head and make it wider; it needs hitting now, and probably did at an earlier stage!

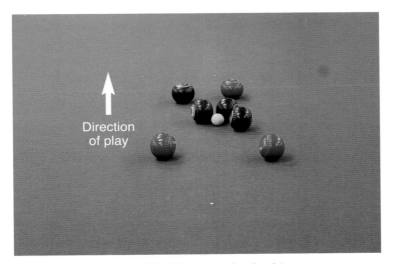

You have to start hitting heads like this sooner rather than later.

However, in most instances, you will be looking for an ideal result from both of your deliveries as a skip in fours. Again, this correlates with the need for 'playing the percentages'. There is no point in building up a healthy head if you only have one attempt at getting the ultimate desired result, and, furthermore, no point drawing to something that needs hitting.

Triples play

Remember, if you are playing triples and are skipping, the first delivery as a skip is almost like a number three's last delivery. The first bowl from the skip in triples can be used to improve the head in some way, even if it is not the perfect result and just helps you for your next two bowls.

At two in triples, you are playing two positions, as bizarre as it sounds. You are playing at two and at three and thus must act accordingly: you must provide the aforementioned backbone. Again, head-building will be an essential skill you must perform, as well as showing sensible tactical nous and being able to play the full range of shots. Again, the number two position, even in triples, is arguably the most difficult position to play.

Lead

The lead in triples should just do what he/she does best (getting them close), but if two of the bowls are around the head I strongly believe that the third delivery must finish behind the jack in a good receiving position, if it misses the intended target of resting off a bowl, trailing the jack, etc.

26 Tactical Approaches Indoors

Okay, many people will believe that tactics don't change indoors to outdoors, and vice versa. The object is to get your bowl as near to the jack as possible, and if you are shots down you may have to play a running bowl to get the desired result.

If it were all that simple then the overall result would always be based solely on ability, whereas we know that isn't the case.

Speed and line indoors

Most indoor surfaces run at approximately seventeen to eighteen seconds. Putting it bluntly, that's very fast for most people. Just a little extra 'flick' in your delivery and you could find you have added three or four yards, and I believe that it is very easy to over-adjust indoors, so there is a very good chance that your next delivery will be too short if your last was too heavy. This also relates to line – if you are wide with your first delivery, you invariably find yourself overcompensating with your following bowl.

Whilst this is still the same outdoors, I believe you are more susceptible to overcompensating indoors as the margins can be so fine between a good bowl and a bad bowl.

A yard heavy

Unless you are immensely talented, if you are within a yard with your first delivery indoors I would not worry too much about compensating with your following bowl – we are talking very fine margins here and it may be better that you replicate the previous delivery, making sure you add *no more* weight than your previous bowl. At worst, you will match your bowl a yard through and leave two decent 'receiving' bowls, and, at best, you may have taken a little bit of pace out and finish next to the jack.

Reaching the head

Indoors, you will bowl short bowls. It is inevitable; it is a touch game and occasionally you will get it wrong. It is important, especially as a front-end player, that you bowl as near to the head as possible. Packing the head and bowling close is evidently of paramount importance, and, of course, it is important outdoors too.

That said, especially when an outdoor green is heavy (which most in the UK inevitably are), I must stress again that short bowls are no good. Thus, reaching the head and 'changing the shape' is the predominant tactic that should be deployed. Building a head is also a very good tactic if the situation calls for it, but if you are too short your bowl will just be in the way.

Playing a yard to two yards indoors

Sometimes, in fact most of the time, playing a yard-on/two-yard shot is very difficult indoors. The top players play it excellently, but it can be hard to find a particular line when playing this type of shot. If it is a shot you struggle with, practise until you become better at it.

Practice doesn't make perfect – it's a myth. But it will make you play better and, just as importantly, increase your confidence when playing a shot.

There is sometimes an irresistible urge indoors, when told to just 'reach up' with a yard or so, to play with about six yards of pace. If the target is hit and you get the result you required, no one ever says anything negative about the shot, but if you miss you hear chuntering, or the old chestnut of 'you're too heavy', from your team-mates and you find yourself apologizing and saying it slipped out of your hand faster than you predicted.

If you feel the urge to play with more pace, maybe because you feel more confident in using a finer line, you should let your skip (or vice-skip if you are skipping), know that you prefer playing with a little more pace.

The other adverse effect indoors, when you are focusing on playing a yard/two yards, is that you focus most of your attention on not playing *more* pace than was instructed. To this end, you will occasionally actually bowl short of the head and incur the wrath of your team-mates to a greater extent than if you would have thrashed at it.

Ultimately, if you feel comfortable playing the shot instructed, that's fine, but if not, it is important you let your team-mates know. If you don't feel comfortable or confident playing a shot, you are likely to fail. Your mind is thus wandering and concentration is arrested.

The main point I am making is that you don't always have to play the prettiest shot available. If you have to think about too many variables, it may be easier to play a more 'uncultured' or 'agricultural' shot and play right through it.

27 Tactics in Singles

Jack length

First and foremost, if, at the start of a singles match, you are struggling against an opponent who has elected to play a three-quarter to full length jack, get him/her off that as soon as you win an end. It may well be their preferred length, and if you change the length you may well capitalize on your opponent's weaknesses.

If you fall into the category of only preferring a certain length of jack, practise every other length during a roll-up. Get to be at least competent in all jack lengths and then you will have more options available to you when you are playing singles and would like to change the jack length.

To illustrate this point, shortly before writing this I had a singles match against a fellow county player and found myself 10–0 down, with my opponent playing a short jack. It was outdoors and I was constantly bowling heavy; I couldn't seem to get it in my head that although it was raining heavily and miserable outside, the surface was still playing at a good pace.

I picked up a single, but it could easily have been a score of four. It took far longer than it should have for me to have got the pace of the rink, but, finally, on that end, I felt I had acquired it.

10–1 down and being battered on a short jack overall, what did I do? I put the mat in exactly the same place and the jack where my opponent had been putting it.

Once I felt I had finally mastered the pace (when I collected the score of one), I felt confident in my ability to get some shots back, playing exactly the same jack tactic as my opponent was playing. I ended up losing the jack again when trailing 10–8, and my opponent threw a longer jack down. What was 'his' jack length was now 'my' jack length! I owned it; I was the player to beat on it. He had to try something else and this automatically put him on the back foot.

If I had thrown a long jack, then both my opponent and I would have been guessing as to the correct pace and line, as the last time we had played such a length was on the trial ends. 10–1 could have easily become 12–1, whereas I backed myself on the shorter jack.

It made my opponent think that it was him who had to do something different, and in this way I managed to get the psychological advantage. I ended up winning 21–18 on a fluke. I then fell at the next hurdle against an ex-England international, 21–15. He had the edge over me psychologically, and probably tactically as well. You win some and you lose some.

Variation

If you really feel you should beat your opponent in a singles match (perhaps you are more experienced, or technically more gifted), I suggest employing the following two tactics, which are effectively opposites of each other:

- Keep the same length and play more consistent bowls than your opponent.
- Play a different length every end.

If you are planning to keep to the same length, I suggest trying a short jack first. Many players seem to struggle on this length, which bamboozles me as it should be easier as you have less distance to throw it.

If playing to the same length doesn't work and yet you should be beating your opponent, I would definitely advocate 'unsettling' him/her. Playing short, then long, then three-quarter, then short, then long, then three-quarter, etc. is bound to upset the rhythm of any player. However, if it upsets your opponent more than you then it is a tactic well worth employing, as you will reap the rewards of adapting better with a favourable scoreline.

It is an underplayed tactic, and the sporadic jack lengths could be construed by the opponent as an underhand tactic or something that is making fun of or demeaning him/her. However, this couldn't be further from the truth; it shows that you have had to really think about the jack length tactic and do something different to obtain your ultimate goal – to win.

As the underdog

Rile your opponent. 'One to me? Oh, I thought I was two down, ha ha!' Comments like this at the completion of an end are bound to wind your opponent up, and make him/her feel like the world is against them. If you can get it into your opponent's head that you are clueless and fluking your way to victory, it will rile him/her more and be detrimental to their game.

Make the most of the chances you get. This sounds blatantly obvious, but if you have a conversion shot to make four then play it, *and do not miss!* Complacency may have set in with your opponent and there is a good chance that they will not focus all of their attention on getting successful conversion shots and thus miss proportionately more than normal. As the underdog, if you punish your opponent, you have a chance; if you don't, you will lose.

Don't be short when you are shots down; if you reach you have a chance, but if you are short you are destined to fail. It is important to recognize that, if you are the underdog on paper, you must take your chances.

As Ian Maynard explains, you need to 'risk to win' in sport and, as the underdog, this is exceptionally important:

> One of the concepts I work with is called 'risking to win'. For me, there is a time and place, and it will probably only be two or three times in a match - or maybe just once - and you have to commit to it.
>
> Another saying I use is that it is better to be 100 per cent committed to the wrong shot than it is to be 80 per cent committed to the right one. Ultimately, if you are not 100 per cent then there is some doubt in there and this will transfer to your arm.
>
> This comes back to the 'think box' and 'play box' areas. I call it the 'commitment line'. You have these two boxes and this line right in the middle of it. It is part of the process of stepping over one line and into the other. It is here where you step over the imaginary line and this is the commitment line, where you have decided on your shot and are fully committed to it.
>
> Commit, be bold and 'risk to win'.

Teamwork

28 Introduction to Teamwork

Chiming with the analysis in the psychology section about how to get the most out of your team, there has never been so much emphasis put on how to make a harmonious unit in a team, especially at international level, but this is highly applicable to all levels in the game. In this chapter, I will use other experts' input and my own to show that, without a successful team ethic, you will fail sooner or later.

In the 2012 World Championships, Australia was exceptionally successful. Scotland and Australia claimed all the gold medals between them.

Bowls Australia National Coach Steve Glasson OAM put the team's success down to a combination of positivity within the group and a great work ethic by his players. He very kindly wrote the following key points that make a group of individuals a team.

What makes a team a team?

The age-old question – what makes a team a team? Or, more to the point, what makes a team a great team?

These are just some of my thoughts:

1. Respect

Everybody *must respect everybody else in the team. While some teams often have similar type characters in their midst, we all have our own unique, individual, quirky, funny and sometimes annoying habits to others. It's respecting these differences and embracing them in a positive manner which is vital to having a successful team. I always reckon these unique traits 'make the individual'!*

Respect also includes respecting yourself – the role you have to play, the opposition, your name, the jersey you have on your back, etc!

2. The team

The team always comes first! Know your role and do it to the very best of your ability. Plan well, train well, communicate well. Identify and value the role you have specifically within the group and make it your own.

Steve Glasson, a great player in his own right, believes there are seven focal factors in making a harmonious team.

3. Enjoyment

If it is no longer fun, then get out. You need down time, laughs and relaxation. Who wants to get up and go to work for and alongside cranky bosses and workmates? Bowls is no different!

4. Confidence – not ego

If there is one thing I can't tolerate, it's arrogance! In order to be successful, one needs to be talented, gifted and have very high work ethics ... these traits breed confidence. Arrogance is another matter and arrogant people can destroy the culture within a team because it usually turns out to be that it's 'all about them!'

5. Support

Treat your team-mates the way you would like to be treated. More often than not in a team environment, you have to put yourself out a little bit. Support your team-mates sincerely and wholeheartedly. They will not always be at their best and I'm pretty sure you won't be either.

6. Belief

Believe in one another. Your hard work in training will help with belief. Be mentally strong.

7. Legacy

When your time comes – and it will – make sure your legacy is one you can be proud of and others will admire you for all your efforts. You will make mistakes ... don't do them on purpose and learn from them. Take responsibility for your actions.

These seven key points expertly written by Steve are imperative for a successful team/rink at *any* level! This talk really is not just for the elite players. It is this misconception that 'they' play a different game that stops a club bowler from improving his/her game.

Willie Wood believes the ingredients for a good team atmosphere are very basic:

It is essential that you are compatible, including getting on well with each other, rather than it being purely about your style of play. You also have to understand each other's game, including your team-mates' strengths and weaknesses and play as a team – you are all in it as one. It is important that you are friendly on and off the green as that can make the difference.

Goals, roles and communication

As Ian Maynard makes clear, principles of teamwork are inextricably combined with a psychological requirement to fulfil our own needs and that of the rink as a whole:

> There are three things that I call 'goals, roles and communications'. What are my individual goals in terms of playing lead or skip, etc? After the individual has addressed this, then we have to decide what our team goals are – this could include behavioural attitudes.
>
> The roles are what you are expected to do in your position. If you're leading, it's as simple as putting your first two close! However, there may also be off-rink roles – maybe the lead or another player looks after the drinks? It is important that these roles are defined. If you don't know your roles it can lead to anxiety and stress – resulting in a detrimental performance.
>
> The last one is communication. What are we going to say? How are we going to say it? When are we going to say it? This is usually done by knowing the individuals in the team. Somebody might prefer a whisper in their ear, another person might be loud and want the whole team applauding their good bowls, so it is about understanding the needs of the different individuals.
>
> You need to answer those questions up front rather than finding out on the day.

You must know your rink, not just *think* you know your rink.

29 Etiquette Towards Your Own Team

Be polite when playing – but don't be too polite. Don't say 'well bowled' to garbage; that's false, and doesn't help make the player feel better.

Etiquette works on many levels. First, if possible, I would ensure that, as a player, I got to the venue in plenty of time, as no one wants to panic about a player not turning up. However, as explained earlier in the book, this isn't always possible, as many people can come straight from work, so conversely, if a team-mate does come in late, then go easy on him/her. There is probably a very good reason why the player is late and the last thing he/she wants to hear is you moaning about punctuality.

Making your team-mates feel good and relaxed is an essential tool to ensure harmony in a rink. To this end, if you emanate positivity, it will be infectious.

I suggest that you just speak to your fellow players how you would in any normal circumstances and don't get on their backs. In short, talk to them how you would like to be spoken to. No one means to bowl a bad bowl and a bit of reassurance from a team-mate can make all the difference.

If you believe one of your players isn't concentrating as much as he/she should be, I would advocate having a quiet word, but be careful as that may be the way that particular player counteracts any nerves he/she may feel – you have to weigh up whether your actions could make that player's performance worse, and consider whether it could make you playing together in the future untenable.

It's common-sense stuff really. Be positive, not false. Instil confidence and be courteous. Ensure the team is at harmony with one another.

30 Positivity

Positivity in a team has already been considered with regard to how it can psychologically aid an individual and team. However, in my opinion, it is very important that you pursue a positive team ethic in order to enhance both individual and overall team performance.

Positivity encompasses two aspects:

- Positive talk to your team-mates.
- Positive outlook on the game.

I wish to focus mainly on the latter of these two points, as the former has already been explored, but they are also inextricably combined. There is no point in bemoaning your lack of luck or what appears to be your opponent's excessive fortune in getting the desired result. You have to ask what the point is of high-lighting your bad luck and your opponents' good luck. There is none! All it does is let off steam and work as a temporary fix for your sorry state of mind. By complaining, the luck doesn't magically change, and you need to ensure that your focus is solely on getting closer to the jack than your opponents.

We all do it – even the best bowlers in the world (mentioning no names) will spend a considerable amount of the game complaining about their team's lack of fortune and the excessive luck of the other. It is a mindset that is not used in any other sport and I would strongly urge that bowlers curtail this urge to be so pessimistic all the time.

So, how do you have a 'positive' outlook on the game? First, as explained earlier, you cut *all* negative talk out – 'I'm not finding it today' – 'They're playing with this/that type of bowl' – 'They're getting all the luck' – 'You can't play against that' – 'He's a left-hander' – 'We might as well give up now and get a drink'.

Negativity breeds negativity – by using such terms you feel the world is against you and you will not play as well.

Using language such as 'You'll get this' – 'Superb try' (if it was a good effort) and just generally talking in a positive manner will put you in the right frame of mind to sort out whatever problems you have.

By having a positive outlook on the game, you are automatically talking to your team-mates in a positive way and thus you are killing two birds with one stone.

Look at the examples below and what you could say or do instead:

– **Negative:** 'Ha – missed by a millimetre again.'
+ **Positive:** 'Great try.'

– **Negative:** 'You're tight/narrow/short/heavy.'
+ **Positive:** *Don't say anything – you are not helping!*

– **Negative:** 'It's all against us today.'
+ **Positive:** 'Now is the time for us to come back!'

What hope have you got if you have a negative outlook? Skips and number threes should take inspiration from this and understand that your negative attitude could rub off on your team-mates, like a disease.

31 A Team Game

Play for yourself and you will be disliked. Furthermore, you will fully deserve the bad name you get.

As sport has moved forward in general, so has bowls (to an extent). Gone are the days of sole authoritarian control by the skip in fours, triples and pairs.

The lead is as important as the number two, and they are equally as important as the back-end.

If you're still playing skip solely as an authoritarian – stop doing it and learn and listen from the best players! None of them play like this anymore. Yes, the skip has the final say, and that should remain to keep some structure to the rink and a voice of authority when it is needed in a game, but, ultimately, the game has moved on.

Your mindset needs to be conducive to you feeling comfortable as an individual, but also acknowledging that you need to tailor it to ensure that you are compatible with your team-mates. Ian Maynard explains why this is so important:

> Getting the right mental attitude differs from individual to individual. It is about understanding what works for you. This can often be a problem in pairs, triples and fours as you will have four different people trying to bowl as a team. You have this fine line between what you need as an individual and what you need as a team member. It's about fulfilling your own needs and, by the same token, you have to be a part of the team. Because of this there are some small compromises to be made because your team would be that much stronger for it.
>
> It is very much about making it specific to the needs of the individual as well as the needs of the team and you may have to slightly tailor your style of play to suit the team. That said, it might be that, when it is your turn, the rest of the rink say, 'Right, you do what you have got to do', but for the rest of the game between deliveries and so forth, you will have to adopt the team approach.

This balance must be met in order for a positive team ethic, with members playing to their ability, to prevail.

Furthermore, it is essential that the team is on the same wavelength. When a skip goes down to bowl, it is imperative that the rink is united, as stated by David Bryant, using his old team-mate David Rhys Jones as a great example of saying the right thing at the right time:

> If you haven't got anything constructive to say, keep your mouth closed. If it's a competitive match and you are under pressure, that is when the solidarity of the four is worth its weight in gold. They know when their team-mates open their mouth, it will be constructive.
>
> Nobody wants doubts in their mind when they go to the mat. When I played, we would all be in agreement and when I went down to play, David Rhys Jones would clap his hands and say: 'Come on then. You can do it - we're with you!' That is the most important thing of all.
>
> What you don't want when you go back to play the shot is the third to say: 'I think you should have come that hand ...' or tell the rest of his team: 'He's on the wrong hand, he won't get this'. You sink or swim together. The skip decides what shot to play and everybody says, 'Go and do it'.

32 Playing the Skip's Role

Although, as has been made abundantly clear throughout the book, the skip should not be some dictator wafting his or her arms around and playing the role of sole authoritarian, there may come a time when such an approach is needed in a game. However, doing this after spending the majority of the game listening and taking in instructions may leave the rink bemused and upset. It is because of this that there needs to be a pre-match dialogue to explain that this could possibly happen. Ian Maynard categorizes sportspeople in three ways - autocratic, democratic and *laissez-faire*. You may adopt all three styles in one game, but it is vitally important that your team-mates know this may be the case:

> There is a time and place for each of those individual styles. When one person has got one shot to win the gold medal, it is probably the

time to be autocratic, as long as your rink know what you are doing and why you are doing it.

There will also be a time to be democratic – when everyone should get some input. For some, it may be that match-winning bowl but for other skips it may be that the skip tells his rink that they don't need any input.

Tony Allcock explains that there may be a time and place to adopt a different management style in the rink, but the crucial thing is that you know the players and they can respond to it, otherwise it will be detrimental to overall performance:

You can liken it to an artist. An artist will know when to apply a certain type of paint at a particular time. A good commander will know what strengths and weaknesses lie in the team and can utilize them accordingly.

For example, I was never a big driver. I resisted driving. I would much prefer a timing shot than a full-out drive.

The skip needs to know how his team-mates want to be handled if they're playing badly.

I remember playing in the national fours final with a very young rink in Andy Wills, Les Gillett and Simon Jones, and we were 19–5 up but they were playing lousy. I got them in the middle and gave them a rollocking and we didn't play the last few ends because they improved and they needed that to get them to play well again. At 19–5, I drew shot to save a six because they were just thinking about the trophy and it was all too much, but I knew them and I could do it with them.

This worked. Tony knew them. However, in doing this, you must be sure that you know the rink well enough and are sure it will have a positive impact, not a negative one.

David Bryant believes compatibility in personality, goals and overall objectives is fundamental to a harmonious team:

As a skip, you've got to get your rink's trust and confidence. Good 'tactics' off the green can help. You can learn a lot by talking to top bowlers.

You need to find compatible players. I was enthusiastic about the game and so was David Rhys Jones and we could talk for hours about bowls. This is one of the reasons why we teamed up in the first place.

You learn a lot by experimenting, but, whatever you do, don't experiment in the middle of the match.

By talking, you also get to know more about each other and each other's game.

It's important you know your rink with regards to style of play but also personalities as well.

It's obvious, but compatibility is essential, otherwise, eventually, a crack in the armour will be exploited by your opponents and you will fail.

33 Your Opponents

'My word – these guys are relentless. How have they pegged us back so much and how are they so positive *all of the time*?'

This is what your opponents should be saying about you. Positive work within a team will be noticed by your opposition, and they have two choices to make:

- Take your example.
- Fold and relent.

If you have a good start to a game and your opponents aren't in the right frame to dig deep and get back into it, and you clearly show through your attitude that you will not relent, you are already on the way to a positive result.

There are scenarios that can scupper this positive mindset. For instance, a large score from your opponents can alter this positivity. There is no point having a great, positive outlook during a game simply until you face an adverse situation. This is when the rink needs to rally (or individual in singles) and move on from that negative result and continue to play with a positive frame of mind until the very last end.

A positive frame of mind is *always* important, but if you see it evident in your opponent(s), it is incredibly important that you replicate this. You may be more naturally gifted than them, and get over the line even with a negative attitude but, ultimately, you will perform far more strongly as an individual or a team if you don't take the attitude that everything is against you or that you would rather be somewhere else.

Physical

34 Introduction to Physical Activities

Warm-up routines, particularly before a match, are *finally* becoming more prevalent in the sport of bowls, though there is still a long, hard, rocky road to go before it is accepted as general practice.

Some top-class players are implementing basic warm-up routines before a match to aid them physically and psychologically.

As Commonwealth Games singles champion Natalie Melmore emphasizes, it gets you in the right frame of mind to play and makes you supple and ready for play, and can be a good way for a team to bond:

> If we are frank, looking across the board at the top bowlers around the world, there are not many who would appear to be at the peak of their physical fitness. So the question is, why do I choose to keep fit and ensure I am physically prepared for every game? For me, bowls is a sport based largely around concentration and mental toughness.
>
> However, your physical abilities will make a huge difference to your performance in a game, particularly when you are playing multiple fixtures in a day. To play a game when your muscles are feeling tight or you are tired will distract you from the necessary focus you require to play at your best.
>
> Stretching before every game is beneficial. Irrespective of the physical benefits, within a team this allows for excellent bonding and will prepare everyone mentally for the game ahead. We are all guilty of turning our noses up at new practices within the game, and stretching often still falls under this umbrella.
>
> If I ever begin a game feeling mentally 'under par', then I am extremely unlikely to perform at my peak. It is extremely important to recognize any particular needs your body has and ensure that you have a personal way of tackling or dealing with these. Personally, I have a knee injury so must ensure that I have stretched and strengthened this area before I play, otherwise, my delivery is affected.
>
> 'If it ain't broke, don't fix it' does not apply to stretching. If it might have a positive effect on your game, then why not give it a go?

I agree with Natalie's view that top-class players who don't warm-up before a game are missing out on maximizing some of the finer details and are putting themselves on the back foot straight away. It is also a good way to get into a routine with your team-mates if you do a warm-up together before a game.

However, it must be stressed that in no way is stretching and doing physical exercise an 'elitist' undertaking. It most certainly does no harm, and I would suggest it does a lot of good for all bowlers to do some simple, gentle exercises, if only to improve their general well-being.

I'm not suggesting that you go and get yourself a personal trainer and implement a rigorous and gruelling fitness regime to help you achieve more in the sport of bowls, but I think that gentle exercise can markedly increase the standard of your overall performance.

In this section I rely heavily on the expert knowledge of Rex Hazeldine, who is in the Sports Coach UK Hall of Fame for his work in a number of sports, including rugby for the England team and women's hockey at the Olympics, and is also a Level Two coach in bowls. He explains that physical exercise is not only important physiologically but also psychologically.

As sports scientist for Bowls England, he is at the forefront of the fitness regime employed by the England team for international series events, World Championships and Commonwealth Games, and the simple advice he imparts in this book should be beneficial to everyone.

I attended a training day for junior internationals where Rex put particular emphasis on how a set of warm-up exercises can have a positive impact on your performance.

Before the first game we did some very simple mobilizing and stretching exercises – the usual – calf, hamstring, etc. All of the stretches made our bodies more supple and we were ready for action straight away.

We went in for lunch after the game and went straight back on the greens after without a warm-up and it was noticeable that the quality of play was of a considerably lower standard than before.

General exercise

As well as doing a warm-up routine, it is also important that you remain generally as fit and healthy as you can. A warm-up routine before a match will certainly help you, but regularly exercising muscles as a general practice will bring about better fitness benefits.

We put a lot of strain on a number of areas when we bowl. Repeating a delivery for up to eighty-four times in a game (potentially more in a singles match) and doing this numerous times a week will eventually take its toll.

Rex Hazeldine has some excellent advice that will help you get a warm-up regime to help you play better bowls.

I will only explore a few exercises here as I am fully aware that this topic could become a bit dry otherwise. Obviously, when doing general exercise, you don't need to go down the club and go on the green to perform them. The illustrations that follow are only for show.

The areas of the body that mainly take the stress in a bowls match are the spine, lower back, shoulders, hips and abdominal region.

A push-up is a simple exercise which can help to strengthen your shoulders and help condition you to be able to cope with the strains of repeatedly delivering.

Strong abdominals will support your lower back; thus exercising to

Push-ups strengthen the shoulders.

Sit-ups can have a positive effect on your general state of health. One way of performing a sit-up is by crossing your arms.

You can perform a sit-up with your hands by the sides of your head if you prefer.

strengthen them will have a knock-on effect in other areas of the body. The best-known exercise to help the abdominals is the sit-up, also known as an 'abdominal curl'. Lying on your back with your knees bent and your hands across your chest or resting on your head, raise up and touch both knees with your elbows.

When I explore what would be ideal for a warm-up routine, bear in mind that those exercises would also be very useful as general stretches and exercises to perform at any time to increase your general fitness.

35 Is it Worth Doing a Warm-up?

It is definitely worth doing some kind of warm-up routine to aid you physiologically, and also psychologically.

There is no need to get involved in the finer details of how stretching can improve your performance; just implement Rex Hazeldine's suggestions and I will be surprised if you don't hit the ground running. You will feel good, you will feel supple, you will feel prepared and, if your opponent has not prepared accordingly, you will feel that you already have the advantage.

You may still be a sceptic, or feel that you are not capable of doing such a strenuous routine if your joints aren't as supple as they used to be, but I would suggest that just the very simplest stretch could help you, and could actually decrease the chance of injury during a match.

Indoors, you are unlikely to suffer any major muscle damage, but outdoors is a different matter. If you are not physically prepared for a match, this can have consequences, as Rex explains:

> There is evidence to show that doing a warm-up will help to reduce the chances of injury.
>
> When you deliver a bowl, the muscles have to stretch. I know it is a fairly gentle movement but nonetheless there is still movement in the joint and muscles do stretch when you go to deliver a bowl. You can reduce the chance of injury by warming up the muscles and increasing the blood flowing through them, increasing their elasticity.
>
> If you are relatively elderly, your muscles and joints are pretty stiff, so to do a bit of a warm-up routine would be beneficial.

Ultimately, if you still think that this is something that will not be of use to you, all I can ask is that you just give it a go. There is a chance that it will be beneficial to your game and it will also make you look as though you mean business.

Your general health is also important. You should strive to have a certain level of fitness because this will have a significant impact on your endurance. Asked whether it is worth exercising as a bowler, Rex states:

> My argument on this resonates around endurance. The prolonged nature of bowls means that it is an endurance sport because it is played over two to three hours generally. If you enter tournaments you may play for a couple of hours, finish your game, have a rest then come back on for another couple of hours. It takes longer than a game of rugby or football, but obviously the intensity is less.
>
> The other factor that I would add is that you always want to delay the onset of fatigue in sport. The better your overall fitness, the longer the delay of fatigue. From research that has been done, we know that fatigue affects co-ordination, concentration and performance. Taking that into account, what kind of condition do you want to be in when it is the twentieth/twenty-first end and your one bowl could make all the difference? Obviously you want your level of fatigue to be as low as possible.
>
> The cardiovascular system also has a role in regard to regulating body temperature. If it is a warm day, not only does the body have to provide energy to play bowls, it also has to adjust your circulation to keep your core temperature down.

Thus there are a number of reasons why a bowler should strive to have a good level of endurance fitness, and to say that your fitness has no impact on your performance is clearly false.

36 Physical Workouts Before a Match

A physical warm-up can be part of your 'routine' before a match. It should always be the same time after time and can do your body and mind immense good, from the very start of the match.

Rex Hazeldine explains the importance of warming up to get the circulation working and your blood going to all the right places:

> There should be a little bit of walking around for a warm-up. You want to increase the body temperature and the blood flow through the muscles. Physiologically, there needs to be a redistribution of blood.
>
> For example, after a meal, or when you are sitting down, a lot of blood flow goes to the abdomen and the kidneys and the liver to deal with all of the digestion.
>
> When you're thinking and writing, blood goes to the brain. Not a lot of the blood supply goes to the muscles because the body says to itself that the muscle mass isn't doing anything so there's no point of sending blood and oxygen to the muscles.
>
> So when people first step onto the green and haven't done a warm-up, there is a limited blood supply. With a warm-up, you are sending a message to the body that you are about to do something physical and you are redistributing the blood flow to the muscles where it needs to go.
>
> Do some easy walking in different directions with gentle movements. Just loosen the joints. You don't really have to run.

Rex explains that the reason why we bowlers haven't done physical routines in the past lies somewhere within the 'culture' of the game:

> You can justify it physiologically, but people think it's strange. Within the culture of bowls, we don't ever warm-up and stretch. Anyone doing some sort of stretching routine will be looked at strangely because a warm-up has never been in the culture of bowls, whereas in almost every other sport that you can think of everybody does a warm-up routine. This is one of the reasons why there is a debate as to whether bowls is a recreation or a sport.
>
> I'm not sure at club level whether it is justified, but at the higher levels, a warm-up routine will aid your preparation so you 'hit the ground running'.

Just because we haven't done it in the past does not mean we can't strive to change the 'culture' in the sport and implement it for the future.

Types of exercise – mobility exercises

As well as walking and jogging to get moving, you can also do simple joint movements to enhance your workout. Lifting your knees high up and from side to side will aid you in a light workout. The idea of doing mobility exercises is to increase body temperature, blood flow and mobilization.

Small, regular movements will increase the blood flow to the muscles.

Do this for the left leg and the right leg as you jog or do a fast walk.

Types of exercises – flexibility exercises

Stretching is essential to get the muscles and joints moving. Ideally, you will have plenty of preparation time to get the muscles warmed up, but just five or ten minutes can make a noticeable difference.

This helps the gastrocnemius calf muscle.

Calf muscles

You use the calf muscles every time you deliver a bowl. To exercise the calf muscles, put one foot in front of the other as shown in the picture. Bend the front leg and keep the back leg straight. Keep the heels of both feet on the floor, with the toes pointing straight ahead. Obviously, repeat with the other leg.

The calf muscle other than the gastrocnemius is the soleus, which can be stretched by keeping the same stretch as before but lowering the hips so that the knees are now bending slightly. Again, it is important that the heel is kept down.

After doing the calf exercises, it may be a good idea to get back into more mobility exercises - walking and easy jogging.

By bending the knees slightly, you are now working the soleus muscle in the calf.

Hamstrings

The easiest way to stretch the hamstring is by placing one leg slightly in front of the other. It is the one in front that you are stretching this time. Bend the back leg, and put your hands on the bent back leg. Keep the front leg straight.

This is the easiest way of stretching a hamstring.

Quadriceps

To stretch the quadriceps (quads), stand near something if you struggle for balance. Flex one knee and raise your heel to the buttocks, preferably so your foot just touches the buttock, but make sure you don't over-compress the knee. Keep this in position for about ten seconds and then change to the other leg.

Working the quads is good as part of a pre-match warm-up routine.

Triceps

To help further with your warm-up, I would certainly advocate warming up the triceps, as every time you deliver you will be reliant on these. With your arms overhead, hold the elbow of one arm with your other hand as pictured. Gently pull the elbow behind the head and repeat with the other arm.

This is an excellent way of warming up your triceps.

Side

Finally, as a general exercise before playing, it is good practice to stand with your arms above your head and lean from side to side, as shown on the following page.

Side stretches are a good way of finishing your exercises.

37 Physical Workouts After a Match

In most other sports you have a 'cool-down' to ensure you are not going from working your muscles strenuously to doing nothing. Whilst bowls is not as physically demanding as, say, football or rugby, you are still doing a fair bit of exercise by walking up and down and delivering your bowls.

You might think I've lost the plot here. We're playing Drake's fair game, but how many times have you come off the green complaining about some kind of ailment? It happens regularly, and any physical regime that reduces those aches and pains has surely got to be worth doing?

As Rex Hazeldine explains, even though we might not want to cool down, it is just as important as a warm-up:

When you have played it can be hard to then do a cool-down. You've either won or lost and psychologically, the typical cool-down period is not a good time. That said, physiologically, it helps the body go back to normal.

When you finish, there is still lactic acid in the muscles and you have the blood supply still pumping and the heart rate is up and so on, and so it makes sense physiologically, and it has been well proven, to do some light exercises and to do the same stretches, just to help the body recover. The main thing is that you move the lactic acid out of the muscles.

You've got to be doing it within fifteen to twenty minutes of finishing. The cool-down should last between five and ten minutes maximum.

38 Hydration and Nutrition

Hydration

I don't need to be an expert to tell you the importance of hydration. However, it is amazing how much such areas can be neglected by the bowling fraternity.

Indeed, even Tony Allcock MBE admits that he used not to take drinks during the game for fear of it breaking his concentration, and he strongly believes that he lost crucial matches in his bowls career because he didn't hydrate properly: 'I might have lost a game by one shot in the past because I wasn't staying hydrated. Once I'd finished a match, I used to drink a bucket of water because I was so thirsty but now I appreciate the importance of hydrating properly.'

For myself, it is very rare that you will see me playing without some form of liquid at the side of the bank: outdoors it will be water; indoors, water or coffee (this is to keep me awake and alert with the lights and warm atmosphere inside).

Dehydration affects concentration, which in turn affects performance. Rex Hazeldine emphasizes the importance of hydration and the process of getting dehydrated and its consequences:

You don't wait until you are thirsty, because thirst is a very late indicator that you are already dehydrated. Have a strategy of hydrating yourself on a regular basis, even though you don't feel thirsty.

Some forty per cent of bodyweight is fluid. There is fluid in cells, fluid in interstitial fluid around the cells and fluid in the blood. Because the body does everything for survival, if the cellular water decreases, it moves water in from the interstitial fluid, which in turn moves water from the blood. The plasma in the blood therefore decreases, therefore your circulation is affected and thus your concentration and performance is affected.

A two per cent decrease in hydration can make you have a twenty per cent drop in concentration.

The most important thing that you drink is water, but if there is a little bit of energy in that (Lucozade, etc.), you will get a little bit of a bonus.

I feel that getting some water from the side of the bank when you are not playing can also aid you psychologically. Once you have played what you need to play and there is a break in the game as players change ends, etc., I think it gives you something to do and keeps your mind engaged in an activity of some sort without the problem of keeping focus or feeling a kind of boredom as little is happening.

That aside, keeping yourself hydrated will clearly increase your attention and concentration and these are essential factors that will aid your performance. You can be exceptionally talented, but if you allow your concentration to wane, you are susceptible to playing to a lesser standard, which can be hard to get out of and can lead to you having a bad game.

Nutrition

With regard to nutrition, although bowls is not physically exhausting, you are still doing a lot of walking up and down and, depending on your antics on the rink, you could also be doing a lot of running around. It can also be mentally exhausting playing a bowls match, and giving yourself the best chance by eating the correct foods before and during a match will increase your overall concentration.

Thus, and especially when you consider that an outdoor match can last three hours and an indoor match four hours, you need to look at eating things that will be beneficial to your performance over a sustained period: you need to ensure that the food you eat will give you enough energy to concentrate sufficiently.

What you eat in general, and getting the right nutritional balance, is very important with regard to performance. If you get it right it will minimize or delay fatigue when you play, improve your competitive performance and generally make you a healthier person.

Everybody is different and there is no single diet that meets the needs of all players at all times, but a little bit of common sense can go a long way. Bacon buttie and chips? Probably not!

For energy supply, carbohydrate is paramount, but you must ensure that your energy intake does not go above your energy output (i.e. how many calories you take in/how many calories you burn when you play).

Carbohydrates such as pasta, rice, cereals, and fruits such as apples, are good for slow-release energy. These are what are known as 'low glycaemic' and break down slowly, delivering a steady supply of glucose and so would be ideal about an hour before a game.

Bananas give you a quick energy rush and are thus 'high glycaemic'. This would be perfect during a game when you need a quick energy boost. Certain types of sweets and energy drinks provide a similar solution during a game or just before you start when you need a quick release of energy.

I won't go into the finer details of a balanced diet, but will look at what types of foods will be useful before a game. Again, I am grateful to Rex for supplying me with much of this information.

Ideal foods before a match:

- Cereals with skimmed milk.
- Baked beans or tinned spaghetti on toast.
- Toast/crusty bread and jam/marmalade/honey.
- Bagels, baguettes, sandwiches filled with cold meats, tuna, salmon, salad.
- Jacket potatoes filled with beans, cottage cheese, tuna and sweetcorn.
- Rice, pasta and potato salads with bread.
- Low-fat milk/yoghurt shakes or smoothies.
- Isotonic sports drinks.

During the game, anything sugary is very helpful – so chocolate bars, bananas and jelly sweets are particularly useful.

After a game, you may well need further sugary snacks to aid a rapid recovery. Honey, jams and fast-recovery fruits such as bananas would also be beneficial. However, I would personally only condone taking such sugary snacks if you have done a warm-up and cool-down and are making these part of your exercise routine. If not, you could be taking in more energy than you are giving out.

39 How a Physical Routine Can Aid You Psychologically

If you feel fully prepared and more supple, you can really hit the ground running. To this end, a physical routine can provide invaluable psychological assurance and give you that extra confidence that you will be able to perform to the best of your ability, time after time.

A healthy body will make for a healthy mind and so, by doing a simple physical routine before a game, you will feel, in my opinion, more focused and ready to tackle the task in hand.

As well as physical benefits, there are certainly psychological values about going through a warm-up routine before you start. As Rex Hazeldine explains:

> While you are doing these physical stretches, you can find your own space and it helps you to concentrate and visualize, going through various psychological strategies. It works in well with psychology because when you are doing physical routines, it helps to keep you relaxed, to build up your concentration carefully, and it marries in the physical and the mental.
>
> At Delhi, all the members of the England Women's squad regularly stretched off and warmed up before all their matches, which they all found beneficial.

This is the end of the physical section. I hope it has been useful and that there is something for you to take away and contemplate.

Conclusion

40 How to be Half Monk, Half Hitman

In *Casino Royale*, James Bond attempts to sum up what his job title entails to M by uttering: 'So, you want me to be half monk, half hitman?' Little did he know that he was also summing up how to be the perfect bowler. To be the perfect player, you have to effectively be the embodiment of this paradox. You have to be polite, courteous, a great team player and get the most out of your team-mates, but you also have to be extremely focused and ruthless in the execution of your shot.

David Rhys Jones was a team-mate of David Bryant's for many years. The pair met in the early 1960s and were bowls partners for over twenty-five years. Here, David Rhys Jones gives his insight as to why David Bryant was one of the greatest players in the history of the game (if not *the* greatest player), and why he embodies the half monk, half hitman principle.

I am often asked what made David Bryant so special. Indeed, the author of this publication has just bearded me with the very question.

Where can I start? What made him stand out from the crowd? What was the secret of his success? Was there a magic formula? Did they break the mould when they created the 'Greatest Bowler Who Ever Lived'?

Like the philosophical arguments that rage over whether it's nature or nurture that shapes our destiny, we could dwell for a decade or two on a whole range of factors that are prerequisites to fashioning a world-beater in any sport.

Was it technique, tactics or temperament that made DJB special? Ah – the three T's!

I played alongside the rose-growing, trout-fishing, pipe-smoking maestro for more than twenty-five years, so I am probably in as good a position as anyone to answer the question. But I am not sure if I can.

Technique? David was self-taught, and had a style that few have copied. It was hardly textbook, but it worked for him, though that crouch, slow rise, and subsequent descent to launch his missiles was certainly hard on the legs and back.

To be honest, I have seen bowlers with better (or at least simpler,

David Bryant CBE is widely regarded as the greatest player in the history of the sport, and is the embodiment of the 'perfect' bowler.

David Rhys Jones (centre) played with David Bryant for many years: the pair were perfectly compatible.

more easily coachable) techniques – ones that I would heartily recommend beginners to study if they aspire to succeed. But I have never seen anyone with a better record.

Tactics? David had some unusual ploys that worked more often than not. A touch player, he would surprise you by playing long jacks on very heavy greens and short jacks on surfaces that were like glass. He would also vary the length of jack to his advantage – but, then, don't we all?

Temperament? Now we are getting somewhere! If some of the players I have seen with seemingly impeccable deliveries had but a small fraction of David's temperamental armoury, they would be world-beaters.

Most of us give up too easily. Referring to the green, we say: 'You can't play bowls on this'. Referring to the opponent we say: 'We've no chance against him'. Referring to Lady Luck, we say: 'She's deserted us – it's just not our night!'

Not David Bryant! He would regard such difficulties as a challenge, and apply his mind to finding strategies to overcome the obstacles that were in the way.

With regard to his unorthodox delivery, every aspect of it had been thought through, and every feature of the stance, the grip, the step, the follow-through, were intentional – and the product of an active and very analytical mind.

With regard to the tactics, he would respond to the state of the green, or the state of the game, or the perceived weaknesses in his opponents pragmatically – and, glory be, he would find the right answer time and time again.

With regard to his attitude to winning or losing, his competitive instinct was employed 100 per cent to find a way to win. He had complete faith in his own judgement – but he was not dogmatic. If his theories proved unproductive, he had the confidence to change his mind, and would then unreservedly believe he was on the right track. He was temperamentally so solid.

Self-belief is the key to so many things in life – but how can you manufacture it? Quite simply, you can't! But David Bryant did – and did so consummately.

And all the time without losing his reputation as a sportsman. He avoided arrogance, was always polite, and gracious in defeat. He hated losing, but you would never have known that, because he could control his emotions.

An eminent sports psychologist once told me: 'Every great sportsman (or sportswoman) gives himself (or herself) permission to lose!' I was amazed. I didn't want to believe it. But, on giving the radical statement some thought, I could see the sense in it.

Yes, you must want to win so much that you cannot

countenance defeat, but … if your desire to win is so overpowering that you become afraid to lose, you probably will. Tension creeps in when you are under that kind of pressure. A rounded person wants to win very badly – but, as the man says, gives himself permission to lose!

Now, I don't think for a minute that David had bought into that notion. Not consciously, anyway! But subconsciously he subscribed to it, I'm sure.

There was no green too heavy, no green too fast, no green too tricky for him. 'Make things difficult', he seemed to say, 'I will find a way to overcome'. And rubbing his hands together with anticipation, he would set about finding the answer.

He was a good manager, who could get the best out of his rink – normally with tact and humour, but he could be serious, too, as when, in a national triples final at Worthing, we were leading 18–1, and we were taking things so lightly that we dropped three shots on one end. He promptly called his lead and second over, and gave us a pep talk. 'We've got to get those back', he said. And he meant it. There was no more messing about!

People ask me what were his strengths; what were his weaknesses? Of the latter, he had few. Was he best at shots that required finesse – or force? He was the master of both – and of the in-between shot, too – the running bowl.

But what was David Bryant's overriding quality? What was he best at doing?

The answer, quite simply, is winning!

David Rhys Jones' exceptional description of David Bryant ticks all the boxes that the book has highlighted. He had the technical and tactical nous to succeed and also an incredible temperament needed to succeed time and time again at the very highest level.

Tony Allcock explains succinctly that:

You can't copy his mentality or determination. His thinking was unique and it made him the 'greatest bowler that has lived.' He was the embodiment of a winner.

41 Stick to Basics

You could analyse what shot you are going to play or how a green is playing until you go green in the face.

Whilst it is important that shot selection is carefully considered, if you 'over-think', you are running the risk of over-complicating the matter and failing in your endeavour to get the shot.

However, 'sticking to basics' covers a whole range of areas. This also incorporates the technical side of the game.

If you think it will be difficult to get around a bowl on a draw, don't change your delivery to cater for this. This will most probably result in the looping mentioned earlier, which needs to be curtailed.

By all means, change your positioning on the mat to slightly alter the angle at point of delivery, but do not try to be any cleverer than that – in the vast majority of cases it will result in failure if you do.

Keep your tactics simple as well. Play the percentage shot and build up the head. These two things should mean that the possibility of conceding a large score is minimized and that you constantly have bowls to use in and around the head.

Don't over-complicate things. If your delivery is highly complex and you are struggling with it, think about adopting a simple stance – just a foot forward, backswing and release delivery. With this, there are fewer variables that can go wrong.

By keeping things simple you are giving yourself the best chance of beating your opponent.

Furthermore, don't think too much. Keep your delivery simple, keep the way you analyse the game simple and don't get too clever.

David Bryant advocated the KISS principle: 'Keep It Simple, Stupid!'

I heard that principle in Queensland. The players there were interested in my philosophy of the game as I had been very successful over in Australia. They couldn't really understand that, as they very rarely lost matches on their own greens.

Once we'd chatted, they said that I obviously believed in the KISS principle. In other words, the more complicated you make it, the more you can get yourself in the deep end. It's all very well theorizing, but if you don't find that the basic theories you apply work then there's no point in putting theories on top of them. If you base theory upon theory without finding out if that theory is correct and perfect it, you will get utterly confused.

If the KISS principle is the best piece of advice implemented and taught by the legend himself, it is obviously one you should be taking heed of. Keep everything in the game simple and let the bowls do the talking.

42 Never Give Up and Always Remain Positive

You should have got the point by now, but, if not, I will mention it once more: quitters never prosper.

While it is still logistically reasonable for you to make a comeback, you should always keep trying. For instance, if you're ten down in the game with half the match to play, this should be tackled as an exciting challenge, not an insurmountable mountain to climb. What's more, you should make it plain to your opponents that you have the mettle needed to force your way back into a game.

Equally important, if you are going into a game as the underdog, I think it is wise to acknowledge this as it should allow you to play riskier shots in the hope of the maximum result, but in no way should it mean that you go into the game with a defeatist attitude.

As Andy Thomson MBE explains, it's not over until that fat lady sings:

I have played in many games when, on the face of it, things were looking bleak and the deficit too much to claw back. However, if you can make it plain to your opponents that you are not going to lie down and take a beating and that you will fight until the very last bowl, it can actually put some pressure on them and occasionally this will produce the desired effect of a great comeback.

I would urge bowlers of all levels to play with the belief that they can beat their opponent if they play to their potential, and to go out there and show their opponents what they are made of.

I think singles is the most bizarre example where people give up. With the vast majority of singles matches played to 21 shots, you are not down and out until your opponent's score says 21, so, even if you are lots of shots down, you can get them all back by playing better, applying more pressure and changing the tactics during the game.

True sportsmen and women never give up, and the sport of bowls asks for the same conviction and effort for you to prosper.

43 How to be the Greatest Bowler Ever

If you've bought this book and have skipped to this final chapter in the hope that I am about to tell you this, well, I am sorry to disappoint, but I don't have the answers. We can't all be the best, and that is why I have got the best to help me in the writing of this book.

However, I hope that this book has gone some way to help you improve your game. That was my primary target when writing it.

As I write this final chapter I am listening to the Beatles. They state, 'I get by with a little help from my friends', and I hope that some of the expert information from some of the top stars in this book has given you some food for thought about where you could improve here and there and thus improve your overall game.

The advice probably won't make you a world champion, but I sincerely believe that if you try some of the ideas, it will make you a better player individually and in a team atmosphere.

Bowls has been living in the past for too long and I hope that my emphasis on the psychological aspects of the sport, with the help of Ian Maynard, John McGuinness and Tony Allcock, and Rex Hazeldine's invaluable input on the importance of physical activity and the part it can play in improving performance, will open up discussion in every bowls club bar.

Bowls is an amateur sport, and it is played by top-class people, and it is important we adhere to the principles of sportsmanship and conviviality. That said, it also needs to be seen as a sport that can be highly competitive and, even if you are playing a local friendly, your primary target (apart from enjoying yourself) should be to win your game.

I hope this book has been of use and I encourage feedback from anyone who has read it. I hope it improves your game. Try some of my suggestions. If they work, great! If they don't, it was worth a try.

It's over and out from me. Now I need to put into practice all of the pointers I have suggested!

Index